the author's toolkit

4th Edition

the author's toolkit

A Step-by-Step Guide to Writing and Publishing Your Book

Mary Embree

ALLWORTH PRESS
NEW YORK

All inquiries should be addressed to Allworth Press, 307 West 36th Street, 11th Floor, New York, NY 10018.

Allworth Press books may be purchased in bulk at special discounts for sales promotion, corporate gifts, fundraising, or educational purposes.

Special editions can also be created to specifications. For details, contact the Special Sales Department, Allworth Press, 307 West 36th Street, 11th Floor, New York, NY 10018 or info@skyhorsepublishing.com.

19 18 17 16 15 5 4 3 2 1

Published by Allworth Press, an imprint of Skyhorse Publishing, Inc. 307 West 36th Street, 11th Floor, New York, NY 10018.

Allworth Press® is a registered trademark of Skyhorse Publishing, Inc.®, a Delaware corporation.

www.allworth.com

Cover design by Chris Ritchie

Library of Congress Cataloging-in-Publication
Data is available on file.

Print ISBN: 978-1-62153-482-2

Ebook ISBN: 978-1-62153-492-1

Printed in the United States of America

CONTENTS

INTRODUCTION

It has been five years since the third edition of *The Author's Toolkit* was released. At that time we were experiencing what came to be known as the Great Recession—the worst economic downturn since the Great Depression. Economists tell us that we have pulled out of the recession but many industries are still struggling and among them are traditional book publishers and major bookstores.

The economy is not their only challenge. New technology has dramatically changed the way books are produced and sold. And it has put greater power into the hands of self-publishing authors, also called indie authors. Self-publishing is now a viable and sometimes better way of launching an author's career. It will not put traditional publishers out of business but it will change the way they operate. Brick-and-mortar bookstores, which have been hard hit by the new technologies and distribution methods, will have to make major changes, too.

Authors who can't get a publishing deal with an established publisher—or choose not to—have a lot of resources available to help them publish their books themselves. Many new companies have been hastily put together to help indie authors through every aspect of the process, including editing, formatting, publishing, promoting, and selling their books. These upstarts have been diluting the influence and profits of traditional book publishing companies.

By 2014, most of the major bookstore chains were gone. Borders, which was the originator of the book superstore concept and was once the second largest bookstore chain in the United States, closed its last store in September of 2011.

As of this writing, the Barnes & Nobles chain is still in existence. It operates about 700 retail bookstores and over 600 college bookstores. It is considered the largest and most forward-thinking bookseller in the United States. Much of their success has been due to their sales innovations, such as advertising on television, publishing proprietary books, and selling their bestsellers at deep discounts. They also sell both printed books and ebooks online as well as their newest Nook e-reader, which has a 10-inch screen.

Books-A-Million is now the second largest bricks-and-mortar book retailer with approximately 250 stores in thirty-one states.

There are still some major independent bookstores throughout the country that are influential in the publishing industry, not only because they sell quantities of books but because of their reputations of excellent service to book lovers, a friendly neighborhood location, and the loyalty of their customers. Many readers still want to go to their local bookstore to browse. They like to wander through the aisles looking at the covers of the printed books and enjoying the feeling of thumbing through their pages. That's why many people like to frequent libraries, too. Some readers have told me that they just love the smell of printed books. You can't get that when you buy your books online. You can't get that when you read your books on e-readers, either. You can't turn down the pages at the corners and you can't underline interesting passages with a red pen. It's just not the same.

This is why I believe that ebooks can never totally replace printed books, just as television didn't replace movie theaters, recordings didn't replace live music, and an email can never replace a handwritten note, a phone call, or a warm hug.

In this fourth edition of *The Author's Toolkit*, I will report on the major changes in the formatting, promoting, and selling of books. As changes are happening at a breakneck speed, it wouldn't be possible to explain them all. In fact, anything I would write about the book publishing industry might have changed before this book goes to print. I will report on trends though, on changes in the method of copyrighting your works, on the difference between formatting an ebook and a printed book, on looking for a publisher for your book, and on the various methods of self-publishing.

What will not change much in this edition are my chapters on planning and researching, writing and editing fundamentals, the rules of grammar and punctuation, and word usage. These principles change very little from year to year.

This edition goes into greater depth regarding publishing your book yourself, which can entail forming your own publishing company. Self-publishing is easier and less expensive than it has ever been. There are many ways to promote books that weren't available to author-publishers even a few short years ago. And many of them are free, such as Facebook and Twitter. For a small charge you can even have your own website where prospective buyers can learn more about you and your books, as well as where to buy them.

Whether you are seeking a publisher or planning to publish your book yourself, this edition brings the information as up to date as possible in our rapidly changing world. It covers more of the advances in technology that have altered the business of publishing and suggests ways that you can adapt to them.

If you are searching for funding, there is now a rapidly growing crowd-funding industry helping people raise money for everything from donations for art projects to financing for businesses. And, of course, to help you pay for the publishing of your book. In the chapter on self-publishing, I will give you information on who they are, where they are, and how to get in touch with them.

This edition will again cover the basic guidelines on writing both fiction and nonfiction. You'll get some pointers on how to be more objective about your own writing. You will learn what you need to know to prepare a professional-quality manuscript. If you do not want to publish your book yourself, you'll get advice on contacting an appropriate agent or publisher. There are still first-time authors who are turning out bestsellers.

The importance of editing your book in accordance to book publishing standards will be explained in greater detail. As a freelance editor who has edited all kinds of books over a career that spans more than two decades, I have seen a number of common errors that authors make and I can show you how to avoid them. And even though no one can make you a talented writer, you can learn the basic rules and principles of writing that can lift your work out of the mundane and into the professional category. Learning the craft will put you ahead of the pack.

Books will continue to be essential for entertainment and education. They provide information that can help us change our lives for the better. They allow us to escape from boredom. They bring us adventure and comfort, pleasure and solace, imaginary love and vicarious revenge. Most of all, they reveal a new and exciting realm for us to experience, no matter what is going on in the so-called "real" world.

There is no way to overstate the importance of the written word. And we, the writers, are the communicators of the world.

We are the very reason books were invented.

CHAPTER ONE

The Beginning

The beginning is the most important part of the work.
➤ Plato

You have an inspiration. It might have come from an event, an experience, a remarkable person, or a fascinating animal. Whatever it is, it inspired you to write about it. But where and how to start are always the major questions at the beginning. Those are the ones that make us sit and look at the blank page or computer screen for an interminable amount of time, tapping our fingers on the desk instead of the keyboard. Sometimes it's hard to put into words the thoughts and feelings we want to express but that's not such a bad thing. Have you ever noticed that writers who tell you writing is easy are writers who have never been published? If writing isn't difficult at times, it probably isn't very good.

Even if you have written a lot of articles and short stories, you may feel that you are not a good enough writer to write a book. But the principles of writing are the same no matter what you are writing. Talent can't be taught but know-how can. If you have ever written anything—business proposals, technical manuals, doctoral dissertations, essays, poetry, or even a daily journal—you can learn to write a book. Of course, the kind of book you choose to write should match your experience and knowledge of the genre and subject matter. Otherwise, you will have to do a great deal of research before you even begin.

Any story worth telling, any lesson worth teaching, and any idea worth expressing are worth writing about. And if you can tell, teach, or express your thoughts well, you can write a book. So if you have a great idea for a book, there's no time like the present to get started.

Maybe it seems to be too great a task and will take too long to complete. You might be one of those writers who ponders the nuance of every word and takes a long time to get her thoughts down on paper. Well, take heart—Franklin P. Adams, in his book *Half a Loaf,* wrote, "Having imagination, it takes you an hour to write a paragraph that, if you were unimaginative, would take you only a minute. Or you might not write the paragraph at all."

Consider the possibility that you may be an excellent writer who simply needs the discipline to sit down and write. You might take years to write a novel that never gets published but that time won't have been wasted. Throughout the process of writing it, you will be learning things you won't realize you learned until you start to work on your next book. It is an undeniable fact that the more you write the better you write.

You may worry about how to make your book interesting, how to organize it and put it together coherently. If you feel that way, you are not alone. Many first-time authors feel overwhelmed at the beginning. Even those who have done a lot of writing before often have fearful feelings when it comes to writing a book—until they learn the process.

Both writing and editing require large doses of concentration, discipline, passion, dedication, and integrity. And the necessary self-editing of your work requires great attention to detail and a merciless resolve to throw out anything that doesn't advance your premise or story.

Whether or not you are working on a book right now, write every day. It has been said that if you do a thing for twenty-one days in a row, it becomes a habit. In *The Artist's Way,* Julia Cameron advises writing three pages every morning. Those pages don't have to lead to a book, they can be about anything. The important thing is that you establish a pattern of writing.

There are many paths you can take to authorship and I suggest you look into as many of them as you can. Attend writer's conferences, book festivals, seminars, and writing classes. Join organizations where you can network with and get inspired by other writers. Subscribe to writer's magazines and newsletters. Buy books on writing and study them. Read great books by legendary authors. Let them become your bedtime reading. Become familiar with the writing process and learn the rules. Then have the courage to break a few of those rules when they get in the way of what you want to say.

Getting Started

To break the attack of inertia, just start typing the first thing that comes to mind about your idea. Don't be concerned with spelling, sentence structure, or anything else. All you need do right now is make the inspired thought tangible. Get it out of your head and onto a piece of paper—or Word program. Don't worry about how you start it, just make the commitment.

Two things to do immediately are to (1) write a short blurb that briefly describes the story or concept and (2) give it a working title that will identify it. That will be the name you put on the folders you create for the project, such as Research, News Clips, Bibliography, Illustrations, Notes, Endorsements, Biographical Information, Character Descriptions, or any other material you gather or create that relates to your proposed book.

The concept sometimes changes. It may grow, improve, or even move in a different direction from that which you had originally planned. Very likely you will rename it by the time you reach the final draft—and maybe before.

Don't worry if you can't figure out what that first page, first paragraph, or first sentence should be. You don't have to know that now. You might find after you have written fifteen chapters that your book really starts at chapter 5 and you can throw away chapters 1, 2, 3, and 4 or plug them in somewhere else.

There are some tricks to get you going, to help you get *something* down on paper before the day is over. If you plan to write nonfiction you could start by explaining what kind of book it is, why you are writing it, and who will benefit from reading it. If you can convince yourself that there is a very good reason for you to write this book, you'll probably have no trouble going on from there.

If you are writing a novel, go into greater detail about the plot. Then describe your main character and put him into a scene that reveals his personality. Where is he? What is she doing? What is he feeling? Is there something compelling about your protagonist? Many of the best novels are character driven. You must know your protagonist intimately so that you will understand why she makes the decisions she does, why he is angry, how far she will go to get her way, or what he is willing to do to get ahead. What are the limits? Where will your protagonist draw the line?

Your characters tell the story and they will take you to exotic and mysterious places you may never have dreamed you'd go. After you do this exercise, if you feel that you have an interesting protagonist and a story that must be told, it will be easy—well, easier—to continue.

In his book *Double Your Creative Power,* S.L. Stebel suggests writing a book jacket for your novel, thinking of it "as a kind of preview of coming attractions." That's very good advice. I advise the authors I work with to become familiar with the book proposal format or even to prepare a proposal as soon as the idea for a book occurs to them. There's probably nothing more disappointing to an author than to write a whole manuscript and find it doesn't have a chance of getting published. The research that must be done to write a proposal could turn up that information. Another reason to study the book proposal format is to help you focus on your subject and organize your work.

What if you have done all of the above and you are still staring at a blank page wondering what that first sentence of your book will be, the one that you know is only the *most* important line in the entire book? This is not the time to concern yourself with the opening sentence. That may come to you later. The important thing is just to get *something onto the page.*

If you think that you still aren't on track, it may be time to disengage your conscious mind. Walk the dog, wash the car, mow the lawn, plant some flowers, bake some cookies—do anything that shifts your brain into neutral—and stop worrying about it. Then tonight before you go to sleep get very comfortable and relaxed and tell yourself that tomorrow when you wake up you will know exactly where to begin. Convince yourself that during the night your unconscious mind will sort it all out and the next day you will approach that blank page virtually exploding with creativity.

Sometimes this works so well for me that my sleeping mind won't let me wait until morning. It wakes me up in the middle of the night with the answer. I turn on the light, get out the pen and paper that I keep in my nightstand drawer, and write it down in detail. There are times when ideas flash as urgently as lights on an ambulance and I must get up, turn on my computer, and start typing feverishly. I love it when that happens.

Planning Your Book

Do an outline or write chapter headings and a short paragraph on what's in each chapter. Some writers put this information on small index cards and arrange them on a table. They can then see the whole book at a glance and rearrange the chapters if necessary. If you are writing a novel, write character sketches too. Get to know the information, people, location, and events that are involved in your story so that you can confidently introduce them to the reader. Once you have a plan, a road map of where you are going, you are not likely to drift off, become lost, or encounter writer's block.

Have a clear idea of what you want to say and then develop your concept along those lines. But don't be rigid. Let it flow like water in a stream, following its own natural course. Unleash your creativity. You can rein it in later when you reach the point of cutting and editing. Make it interesting. If it interests you, it probably will interest others.

Write a Brief Description

To help you focus on your subject, write one sentence that describes your book. Check bestseller lists to see how they do this. Here are some examples.

The Boys in the Boat by Daniel James Brown. A group of American rowers pursue gold at the 1936 Berlin Olympic Games.

Gray Mountain by John Grisham. A young woman whose promising Wall Street career had been snuffed out by the Great Recession hopes an unpaid one-year legal aid internship will be her ticket back.

The Wolf Gift. Anne Rice takes us to the rugged coastline of Northern California, to the grand mansion at Nideck Point, and explores the unearthly education of her transformed Man Wolf.

Not That Kind of Girl: A Young Woman Tells You What She's "Learned." Lena Dunham writes about making one's way in the world and having the guts to believe that your story is one that deserves to be told.

Brooklyn, a novel by Colm Tóibin. The story of a young woman from a small town in Ireland who leaves the world she's known and moves to Brooklyn in the 1950s.

The Lost Symbol, a novel by Dan Brown. Harvard professor Robert Langdon uses his symbology skills to unravel the mystery of a missing Freemason in Washington, D.C.

Say You're One of Them by Uwem Akpam. A collection of fictional stories portraying the suffering of African children.

Blues for All the Changes by Nikki Giovanni. A collection of intensely personal poems on sex, politics, and love "among Black folk."

Too Much Happiness by Alice Munro. The short story master explores women and their relationships in ten new stories.

There isn't any single way to explain what a book is about. But the above will give you an idea of how you could describe yours. Writing these one-sentence descriptions will help you in the writing process by focusing your ideas and sharpening your point of view. This exercise will also help you later, when you are out there marketing your book. There will be more about this in the chapters on Query Letters and Book Proposals.

There is an organization that encourages writers to get started on their novel and I think it's worth looking into. It is Nanowrimo.org. That stands for National Novel Writing Month, which is November 1 to November 30 of each year. The aim is to write a 50,000-word rough draft in thirty days. Please note, that's a *rough* draft. That means you don't do any editing, don't correct spelling, don't rewrite. Just keep writing. If you are interested in trying it out, go to http://nanowrimo.org and sign up. Then follow the steps they recommend. You will get tips and nudges to continue. They'll help you get inspired with pep talks from well-known authors, and help you keep track of your progress. Even if you don't succeed in writing 50,000 words in that length of time, you might just come up with the beginning of a great novel.

For most of us who possess the soul of a writer, there are book ideas that call us, begging us to write them and bring them out of obscurity. I think it would be sad to reach the end of our days and realize with regret that we never did get around to writing that book—the one that tugged at our heart for so many years.

What is the book that calls to you? Is it nonfiction? Are there valuable lessons you could teach? Is there important information you could share? Is it a family history or an autobiography that generations who come after you would treasure? Is it your poetry that springs from deep within your heart that you've never really shared? Is it a novel that is trying to get your attention? Are there voices inside your brain that long to be heard and stories that only you can tell? Are there fascinating characters only you can bring to life? Will you let them languish mutely within the prison of your mind or turn them loose upon the world to tell their story?

Don't wait for inspiration to get started. Sit down at your computer, dust off your old typewriter, or get out your pad of paper and a pen, and write anything that comes to mind. Then just keep writing even if it makes no sense at all. Get a timer and set it for one hour. Ignore interruptions unless they are emergencies. Don't pick up the phone or go to the door. Keep writing. In that hour, the inspiration will come. I can almost guarantee it.

CHAPTER TWO

Researching

Get your facts first, and then you can distort 'em as much as you please.

➤ Mark Twain

In the above quote, Twain was probably referring to writing a novel. For a nonfiction book it would not be a good idea to distort the facts. But no matter what you are writing, the likelihood is that you will need to do some research on the subject. If you are writing nonfiction, research is essential. No matter how well you know your subject, your memory isn't perfect and, even if it were, there are changes that take place all the time that could make your knowledge outdated. You will have to be sure that your information is accurate, current, and has not already been written about in the way you intend to write it.

Even if you are writing a novel there is likely to be information you will need. For example, suppose your protagonist is a cardiologist. You will need to know something about heart problems, surgical procedures, hospital protocol, and so forth. If the action in your novel takes place in Hong Kong you will have to know enough about the geography, climate, customs, people, and laws to make your story feel authentic. It helps if you've been to Hong Kong but if you haven't been there recently and your story is set in the present time, you'll need to find out what it's like there now. There have been a lot of political changes in Hong Kong in the past few years.

You must be accurate about dates, the spelling of names, historical events, recent developments in your subject field, and on and on. The integrity of your research can make you look like an expert or like a novice.

Where do you find all this information? Before computers, writers used to spend a lot of time in libraries. In addition to public libraries, there are university libraries and medical libraries. I did most of my research for my first book in the library located inside St. John's Regional Medical Center in Oxnard, California. The librarian helped me locate some recent studies that had been done all over the world on the health effects of smoking. Through this research I discovered the differences between male and female addictions to tobacco. So, instead of writing a general how-to-quit-smoking book, I focused on girls and women. And that turned out to be the key to getting my book published. There weren't any books out there that focused on female smokers and the greater difficulties they faced in trying to quit.

I had the background to write it. I had smoked from the time I was seventeen until I was thirty-five. I tried to quit many times. When I was finally able to kick the habit I got a job as a stop-smoking therapist at one of the Schick Stop-Smoking Centers. I later volunteered at the American Lung Association's Freedom from Smoking Program, helping smokers to quit. I had first-hand knowledge of the powerful addiction.

After I had completed the research, written the first three chapters of the book, and a chapter-by-chapter outline, I put together my book proposal and found a literary agent who was eager to represent me. Two publishers made offers on it and I chose the one with the larger advance. I didn't finish writing the book until after the publishing contract was signed and I had gotten the first half of my advance. The book was published the following year (1995) by WRS Publishing, a company that was owned by a medical doctor. They chose the title: *A Woman's Way: The Stop-Smoking Book for Women.*

From that book, which was sold mostly through bookstores, I spun off two other works: *The Stop-Smoking Program for Women,* to be used by therapists in the field, and a booklet called *The Stop-Smoking Diet for Women.* Both were published by HealthEdco and sold mainly to hospitals, women's clinics, nursing associations, and doctors in private practice. The twenty-eight-page diet booklet sold better than the book.

Fortunately for writers, the information highway has been repaved and many more lanes have been added. Here are the major ways to find the data you need.

The Internet

Where we once had to get out of our house or office and go to the library, we can now get just about any information we need over the Internet. There is a caveat, however, to getting your facts that way. Not all of the information is unbiased and accurate. You will have to do the research necessary to check out your sources. And there isn't a friendly librarian sitting inside your computer who will help you through the maze of websites and tell you what to click on.

You still have to know what you are looking for and where to find it, and you must know the integrity of the source. Misinformation is worse than no information at all.

When you are gathering information or doing fact checking, be sure that the websites you go to are reputable. For instance, when I was doing research for my book on smoking, I checked out the American Cancer Society and the American Heart Association websites. I went to the websites of the U.S. Department of Health and Human Services and the New England Journal of Medicine for reports of recent health studies on the effects of smoking. I didn't bother with tobacco companies because I was concerned that they might not give me accurate, up-to-date information on the negative effects of smoking. After all, their bottom line would be adversely affected if people knew the truth.

Internet search engines are amazing. If the information you want has been recorded and is anywhere in the world you will probably be able to find it. It takes a while to get used to search engines if you have never used them before, but there is a lot of help for that, too. If you are accessing the Internet at your local public library, someone there will help you get started.

Most of the search engines use Boolean logic, and understanding it will make your search results faster and more targeted. We can thank British mathematician George Boole (1815–1864) who developed a system of logic over 150 years ago that affects how computers operate today. Of course, he couldn't know how it would be applied so far in the future. His system is used to produce more precise search results by formulating specific queries.

You can get lots of information on Boolean logic and how it works both in encyclopedias and on the Internet but you don't have to know much about the process to start your search. The basic search is fairly easy. You can simply type in a few descriptive words. It becomes a bit more complicated if you want to find exactly what you want without having to scan through hundreds of items the search may retrieve. But once you get the hang of it, you will be amazed at the infinite amount of information you can uncover.

The Public Library

There was a time when you could call the librarian of your local library and ask her to locate, copy, and send the information you are seeking to you. Libraries are so understaffed now, though, that services such as that may no longer be available. You might have to go to the library to look things up yourself. But sometimes it's very nice—and inspiring—to get out of your office or house and go sit among the books. There is nothing like the quiet, stimulating energy of a library.

The librarians will teach you how to use the card file to locate where in the library you will find what you need. They will show you how to use their computer for researching if you don't already know how to do so. There may be reference books in the library that you can't get on the Internet. For instance, *Literary Market Place* (LMP) has a website you can go to but if you are not a paid subscriber only a small portion of the information that is in their huge annual reference book is available to you. You probably wouldn't want to subscribe because both the printed issues of the books and the online subscriptions are very expensive.

Usually you can access R.R. Bowker's *Books in Print* and *Forthcoming Books* on the library's computer. When you start doing research for your book proposal, these lists and LMP will be helpful.

There are many other sorts of research materials available in libraries, such as microfiche of newspapers, clippings and art files, special collections, and back issues of magazines and journals. You can borrow documentary films on DVD and audio books on CD.

Specialized Libraries

Many universities, medical centers, and corporate offices have extensive libraries. Some of them may require you to be connected with the institution in some way before letting you use them, but not all of them have those restrictions. Many of these libraries have books that are not available in a public library or on the Internet. You may find that their libraries are also more up-to-date and carry books, journals, and research papers on subjects that relate to what you are writing.

Reference Books

The New York Public Library Desk Reference contains a wealth of information on just about any subject you can think of. On its cover it states, "The complete resource for quick answers to all your questions." I think that is a bit of an overstatement. I can think of a few questions it won't answer. But it does contain an amazing amount of information. Of course, you can't expect it to go into detail on so many entries. However, if you don't need details, just a quick answer, this reference is excellent.

If you have the printed edition of the *Encyclopedia Britannica* and it is recent, that's great. It is still considered by most experts to be the best encyclopedia available. If not, you can get it and other encyclopedias on CDs that you can use on your computer. They are considerably less costly than the printed versions. Again, it is essential to have a recently published encyclopedia. The information you need may not be in an older issue or may be out of date. Most encyclopedias publish a yearbook every year with updated information and it is a good idea to get it so that you can keep current.

It is imperative for a writer to have an unabridged dictionary. My favorite is the *Merriam-Webster Unabridged.* It is the largest, most comprehensive American dictionary currently available in print or online. It is built on the solid foundation of *Webster's Third New International Dictionary, Unabridged,* and is the best source of current information about the English language. Recently, when I learned that it had a release of new content in October 2014, featuring more than 1,900 new words and 850 new senses across a variety of fields, I had to have it. I believe that if you choose to have only one dictionary, this is the one to get.

I can also recommend *Random House Webster's Unabridged Dictionary.* I have the Second Edition (2001) and I keep it under my desk where I can get to it without getting up.

I love my *DK Illustrated Oxford Dictionary* (2003). It's a big heavy book like the books above, but it has illustrations in color all throughout the book. It's so beautifully done. I enjoy simply leafing through it looking at the pictures. This dictionary is truly a work of art.

Among desk dictionaries, I like the "college" dictionaries published by Houghton Mifflin and Random House. *The Oxford American Dictionary of Current English* published by Oxford University Press is also excellent. Again, make sure you have a recent edition. These, too, have CDs you can download onto your computer. Technology is changing so fast that dictionaries are out-of-date even before they are published. Many dictionaries that came out prior to 1997, both desk and unabridged types, do not contain the words *Internet, website,* and many technological words that are now in common usage. There is more on this subject in the chapter on editing.

A book of synonyms and antonyms is helpful if you find yourself using the same word over and over again. We all have pet words and usually don't even realize it. A thesaurus will help you find new words and different ways to say the same thing. And that will certainly make your writing more interesting. The books I particularly like are *Roget's Thesaurus* and Funk & Wagnalls *Standard Handbook of Synonyms, Antonyms and Prepositions.* Funk & Wagnalls' book was first published in 1914 under the title of *English Synonyms and Antonyms.* The first edition of *Roget's* was published in 1852. Of course, both of these books are updated and reissued every few years but it isn't as important to have a recent issue of a thesaurus as it is of a dictionary.

In late 2009 Oxford University Press released their long-awaited *Historical Thesaurus of the Oxford English Dictionary.* It has 3,952 pages in two beautifully bound volumes. Forty-five years in the making, it is the largest thesaurus in the world and the first historical thesaurus for any of the world's languages. It provides a view into the development of words with similar meaning over time, from Old English to the present day. This is not a conventional synonym finder like *Roget's Thesaurus.* The editors of the *Historical Thesaurus* define a synonym as "strictly, a word having the same sense as another (in the same language)." If you are a word addict, you will want to have this magnificent monument to the English language. With a cover price of £250, or $395 in the United States, it would be a rather expensive addition to your personal research library, but you may find it in your local public library.

There's a wealth of information of all sorts in *The World Almanac, The Information Please Almanac,* and other books of this kind. As an example of the kind of information you may find in an almanac, one edition of *The World Almanac and Book of Facts* contained an article on the transition of power in Hong Kong when China regained control after 156 years of British rule. Since almanacs come out with new editions every year, they will have more up-to-date information than some encyclopedias.

Another reference book of this type is *The Cambridge Factfinder* published by Cambridge University Press. It contains a "collection of bits of information for use in the home, at school, or in the office" and claims to contain more facts than any other book of its kind—over 180,000. The book is divided into what they call "broad areas of knowledge" with sections on the universe, the Earth, the environment, natural history, human beings, history, human geography, society, religion and mythology, communications, science and technology, arts and culture, knowledge (academic study), and sports and games.

Research is tricky and it is hard to define what a fact actually is because there are facts about fictions and fictions about facts. *The Oxford English Dictionary* defines a fact as "Something that has really occurred or is actually the case; something certainly known to be of this character; hence a particular truth known by actual observation or authentic testimony, as opposed to what is merely inferred, or to a conjecture or fiction; a datum of experience, as opposed to the conclusions which may be based upon it."

Good research is important. If you are ever called to explain how or where you got your information, it's reassuring to be able to cite a source to show potential doubters that you didn't make up your facts.

Reference Books Specific to Your Subject

If you write regularly about historical events, medicine, alternative health, animals, the environment, or anything else, it's a good idea to accumulate reference books on these subjects. For example, if you were writing articles or a book having to do with health, you might need a medical dictionary, a family medical guide, or books on nutrition, pharmaceuticals, herbal medicines, and various forms of natural healing. If you were writing a novel involving international intrigue and espionage, you might want to get books on spy craft, or on the CIA, the KGB, and other super-secret government agencies throughout the world.

R.R. Bowker's *Books in Print* would also be helpful. Their books are listed by subject matter as are those on Amazon.com. You can also check the books available in libraries and bookstores. They are placed on the shelves in sections devoted to each subject: "mysteries," "psychology," "computers," and so forth. Bookstore clerks and librarians can help you find what you need and may even be able to recommend specific books.

Newspapers, Magazines, and Trade Journals

Keep up with what is happening in the world on a daily basis. Subscribe to a newspaper, preferably a major one such as the *Washington Post, Wall Street Journal, New York Times,* or *Los Angeles Times*. They may not, however, be unbiased in their reporting, so be aware that you will still have to check your facts. Also subscribe to magazines and journals in your field. They will have more current information on your particular subject than other sources. They, too, may contain organizational bias so it would be wise not to rely on them alone.

Publishers Weekly and *Library Journal* are excellent resources. They review thousands of books a year, most of them new. You can keep up with what is happening in the world of book publishing and learn what kinds of books are most popular.

Literary Organizations

Join organizations that are formed to put people together with similar interests, and try to attend their meetings regularly. There is no way to overemphasize the importance of networking with people in the field you are writing about. They are a valuable source of information, inspiration, and assistance. You will also find out who publishes the kind of book you are writing and maybe even get a referral to an agent or publisher by a member who has been published. You will benefit from the research others in your field have done. To locate local organizations, you could go to the section in the yellow pages of your telephone directory. They may be listed under various categories like "Associations," "Clubs," "Social Service Organizations." The Internet is also a good way to find specific organizations.

Experts and Other Authors

When you need expert advice, go to someone who knows the field and subject well. It could take you hours to get the answer to a question through other forms of research when you might be able to contact experts who will answer your question in a matter of minutes. Most of the time this can be done through email or on the phone and you can record the conversation (with their permission).

Reference books should be kept in your home or office library and replaced (or added to) each time a new edition comes out. Having information at your fingertips when you need it can be a real time-saver.

Researching can be very time-consuming when most of us would really rather be writing, but it can make the difference between producing an authoritative, informed, interesting book, and one that is merely mediocre. It can also, as in my case, make the difference between a book that has a good chance of finding a publisher and one that doesn't have a prayer.

A word of caution: be sure that you don't quote directly from any book without giving attribution to the author and getting permission from the publisher. A few years ago two highly esteemed historians were caught quoting other authors extensively without quotation marks or attributing the writing to the original author. It caused such a stir that both of these historians, whose books were regularly on bestsellers' lists, lost much of their credibility. Their reputations were tarnished and it took a while for them to gain back their standing in their field.

Plagiarism is probably the worst transgression an author can be accused of. Well, maybe being boring is the worst, but plagiarism is the ugliest. Also, without permission to use copyrighted works, you open yourself up to potential lawsuits. If you have any doubts about what you can and cannot use, consult an attorney who is knowledgeable in that area. There is more about this in the chapter on Ethics and Legal Concerns.

CHAPTER THREE

Tools of the Trade

Man is a tool-using animal . . . without tools he is nothing.

➤ Thomas Carlyle

You may feel that the only tools you need to write a book are a pen and a pad of paper. And that may be so. But if you want to be accurate and informed, you will need books for research. If you want to be able to write and edit quickly, you will need a word processor or a computer. If you wish to send your manuscript out to an agent or publisher, it must be a typewritten copy or printed on a laser or inkjet printer. Often, publishers want it sent electronically, that is, over the Internet as an attachment to an email. To be an active player in today's market, a writer should have a computer, a good printer, and access to the Internet—and know how to use them. Without these essential tools, your communication will be severely restricted and your book might remain an idea in your head: incomplete, unrealized, and unrecorded.

At any stage in your writing you can assemble your tools, but the best time to start getting them together is before you begin the job. Think of how it would be if the only planning you did to paint your living room were to buy the paint and the paintbrush. You would soon find that you needed tools to open the paint can and to stir the paint with. After you started painting you'd discover that you needed a drop cloth so that you wouldn't ruin the floor. And you might have to stop and spackle the nail holes before you continued. Planning ahead and assembling all the tools you needed would have helped the process move along faster and more smoothly. The same is true for writing.

Here's a list of some tools to consider getting, with a box for you to check off each one as you acquire it. Keep everything you need close by—in the same room, if possible—so that you don't have to get up and go to another room to use them. Some you may not need or be able to get right now, and some you will already have. High on your list should be Internet access. It will be worth it to pay extra for high-speed access. Many magazine and book publishers now prefer that you email submissions rather than using the post office or UPS. And it's cheaper to send things that way. It saves both paper and postage.

Equipment

Your number one need is a computer with a keyboard and monitor or a laptop that contains all of them. There are several sizes of computers so you don't absolutely have to have a desktop computer that takes up a lot of space. You can get a laptop (also called notebook) computer that has the keyboard and monitor built into it. They usually have thirteen- to seventeen-inch displays, which are smaller than monitors generally used with desktop computers. You can also get a computer cart with wheels so that you can move it around the house. It's lightweight and can operate on a battery so you can carry it to a coffee shop, the park, a library, or any other place where you would like to write. If you want something smaller, simpler, and less expensive you could get a mini-computer, also called a netbook. It is lighter still and has less than a ten-inch screen.

If you refuse to upgrade your thinking to the twenty-first century, you could get a word processor or an electric typewriter (preferably a correcting one). Assuming, though, that you now have or plan to get a computer, you will also need some if not all of the following items:

- ☐ A laser printer. I use my laser black and white printer for most print jobs because the copies cost less than those made on an inkjet printer. Also, the ink doesn't smear when I use a highlighter on the printed page. My laser prints on both side of the page, too. It costs a little more for that kind of printer but it is worth it. Duplex printing saves paper and is handy if you plan to bind the pages or put them into a three-ring notebook. You can also get a laser color printer. However, color laser printers are quite costly to buy and the ink cartridges are very expensive, too. You have to buy four separate cartridges to get the full spectrum of colors. By time you read this, that might have changed. Technology changes so quickly that a book like this (just like dictionaries) can't stay up to date. It's best to look at all of them and choose the one that best suits your needs.
- ☐ An inkjet printer. They are quite reasonably priced now. (Manufacturers make most of their profit by charging a lot for toner cartridges that have to be replaced often.) I like an inkjet for printing color photos because they (most of them) make better color copies than lasers do. The inkjet printer I have now is also a copier and scanner. Very handy.

- ☐ A desk, tabletop, or flat area that is for your exclusive use. There are all kinds of setups but I prefer a two-piece set with one being a desk with drawers in it for small supplies like pens and pencils, stamps, flash drives, staples, note paper, and other handy items. Mine also has a large drawer for legal size folders holding files that I refer to frequently. The companion table is shorter because it's a better height for my computer, keyboard, and monitor. It has shelves under it that I use for the back-up battery in case the power goes off suddenly, for a phone book, dictionary, three-hole punch, and other items I use frequently.
- ☐ A good, supportive, and comfortable chair on casters so you can move it around easily. I prefer one with armrests but there are less expensive chairs that do not have armrests and they work well, too.
- ☐ A file cabinet or portable file box so you can keep your rough drafts, notes, and research information in order
- ☐ A bookcase and shelves to store paper, a paper cutter, office supplies, and reference books
- ☐ A telephone. You will probably want a landline for most of your calls but a cell phone is very handy, too, and many people with cell phones are getting rid of their landline.
- ☐ A fax machine. You might not need a fax as there are ways to send legal documents requiring an original signature through the Internet. You might want to look into this.
- ☐ A scanner so that you can scan photos and illustrations that you wish to include in your book. As I mentioned above, it can be an additional feature of your inkjet printer; some are called all-in-ones.
- ☐ Good lighting. This is essential. There should be a three-way lamp on your desk and at least one other lamp that will light up the room in which you are working.

Books

- ☐ An unabridged dictionary
- ☐ A desk dictionary
- ☐ A thesaurus
- ☐ A book of quotations (I have several)
- ☐ An encyclopedia, either in print or on your computer
- ☐ The latest edition of *The Chicago Manual of Style*
- ☐ The latest edition of *Writer's Market*
- ☐ Any other reference books that will be of help in your particular writing project

Supplies

- ☐ Paper: notepads, laser and inkjet paper, copy paper (less expensive), card stock
- ☐ Envelopes: #10s and #9s (to fit inside #10s), manila envelopes in various sizes

- ☐ File folders (legal and letter-size), hanging folders for file drawers
- ☐ Red pens to mark corrections and changes on your printed pages
- ☐ Black or blue pens for jotting down notes
- ☐ Yellow highlighters
- ☐ An extra ink cartridge for your printer (you don't want to run out in the middle of a project)
- ☐ Computer disks or flash drives to save your work on
- ☐ Stapler, staple remover, scissors, paperclips, scotch tape, etc.
- ☐ A coffee/tea warmer. This is a must for me. In the heat of writing, I often forget about my fuel and it gets cold.
- ☐ A white dry-erase board for notes and reminders can help you stay on track. I have a three-month calendar with my appointments on it. It hangs on the wall just above my computer so that I can look at it often without leaving my desk. It has saved me many times from missing appointments.

Make a list of all the tools you think you will need and get them before you start writing. Not only will it save you time in the future, it will put you in the right frame of mind to write and could assuage that bad habit of most writers: procrastination.

Now you are ready. Start writing. That blockbuster novel may be germinating inside your brain at this very moment. You just might be a creative genius. You might have enormous talent—far more than anyone would ever guess. But to get your ideas down on paper in a presentable form you will have to be more than an accomplished author—you must also be a good craftsman. This book will help you with that too.

Your Time

You need to not only gather your tools and set up your workspace, you need to organize your time so that you can spend at least an hour or more each day writing. Once you get going, you may find that you are just getting warmed up in an hour. Then you may want to change your daily schedule or even your life style so that you can fit in a three-hour writing period each day. That isn't easy to do if you are a busy stay-at-home parent of preschoolers or a business executive who works long hours. But those who are bitten hard by the writing bug somehow find the time. One writer I know gets up at four in the morning and gets in two or three hours of writing before her husband and children wake up. Another has a working space in his garage where he goes after dinner and writes until bedtime. Establishing a routine is very helpful but if that is not possible, then write whenever you get a chance, even if it's only notes to elaborate on later.

It takes dedication and perseverance to write a book. How you prepare yourself depends on whether you are a serious writer or just enjoy playing with words and ideas.

Furthering Your Education

If your goal is to become a professional writer, you may need to brush up on your English or composition skills. You already know how to speak, to read, and to write, and maybe how to use a computer. But to become a really good writer you must understand grammar, word usage, parts of speech, sentence structure, spelling, punctuation, and all the other principles of composition. You probably were introduced to all this in school but maybe you weren't really paying much attention. You may need only to be reminded of what you learned in your English courses. However, if you feel you are lacking in some area of writing, it would be a good idea to take some classes.

You can learn a great deal through books. However, just as no driver's training manual could turn a person into a good driver, no book or manual can turn you into a good writer. A person may know theoretically how to drive but he still has to get behind the wheel and do a lot of driving if he is to learn to drive well. And a writer will have to do a lot of writing to become a good writer. In writing, practice doesn't make perfect because writing has no measure for perfection, but practice will surely make you a better writer.

What writing implement should you use? Whatever works best for you. A woman writer I know who was a touch-typist and could type fast still wrote all of her first drafts in longhand. She said, "I can be more creative when I can feel my ideas flow from my brain, through my fingers, into the pencil and spread out onto the paper."

Another writer told me he wrote with a pencil so that he could erase and make corrections. Soon he realized that he was erasing stuff that was better than his "corrections." After that he wrote with a pen and drew a line through the words he was replacing so that when he reread it he could decide which version was better. Later, he began to write incomplete sentences longhand and then fleshed them out when he typed them up. When he graduated from his old IBM Selectric to the computer, he discovered he could compose right at the keyboard with no loss of creativity. Now he almost never writes anything in longhand. He says that he can type much faster than he writes. "When I'm in a creative rush, my ideas are like butterflies. When I use a computer, I can get my thoughts down on paper quickly, before they fly away and settle upon the next idea."

If you like to think out loud, you may be more comfortable talking into a tape recorder and having someone transcribe it for you. Now you can even dictate your book directly onto your computer with speech recognition software. Then you can print your first draft and start editing and refining it.

CHAPTER FOUR

Writing Groups

Criticism comes easier than craftsmanship.

➤ From Pliny the Elder, *Natural History*

If you are like most writers, you want a place to read your writing aloud and get feedback. You want the camaraderie of other writers. They help you stay interested in writing and they're good for sharing the pain of rejection and for celebrating small victories.

Benefits and Drawbacks

When writers I am working with ask me what I think about writing groups I have to say, "It depends on what kind of group it is." Most of them are probably helpful. But some critique groups can have a negative effect on the participants and a writer can come away from an evening in such a group more confused than before. A friend of mine got so much negative criticism and bad advice from the other members that she left the meeting in tears. It was a scriptwriting group and she was the only one in the group who was a professional scriptwriter. The others had read books about how to write a script but had never sold any. Perhaps she should have let their negative comments just roll off her back, but she couldn't. She told me that she was so discouraged that she stopped writing for a while. Rational or not, her reaction was understandable because I had a similar experience myself.

There are writing groups where authors get together to share their work. They are like support groups where they give each other encouragement and are nonjudgmental. These can be very beneficial. There are critique groups that are put together to evaluate each other's work. And these can be harmful. A synonym for critique is criticize. Often the writers in critique groups are not experienced, have not been published, and may not be good writers themselves. When that is the case, what is the value of their opinion?

When I began working with authors on their books, editing, advising, and guiding them through the process, I realized how destructive a negative comment could be on a writer and I determined to watch what I said very carefully. The last thing I wanted to do was to discourage anyone from writing. Although I may pull my punches and be gentle in my criticism, I am honest and straightforward with my advice to writers. That's what they are paying me for. But I always find something positive to say about their work, even if it needs a lot of rewriting, before I make suggestions about what to change. I tell them what I like in their manuscript, what I think works, as well as what doesn't work. Only rarely will I tell them what they "should" do. Instead of saying, "There is no reason for this character to be in the book. You should take him out," I will ask questions such as, "What is the role of this character? What does he have to do with the protagonist or antagonist? How does he figure into the story?" When the writer analyzes it herself, she will make the decision to get rid of the character or give him some meaningful purpose. I think a participant in a writer's critique group could be more helpful if she asks a question rather than offers an opinion.

I have found that a person learns just as much from positive feedback as from negative criticism—maybe more. When they learn to build on their strengths they automatically minimize their shortcomings. And we all have shortcomings.

Writing groups can be very beneficial. I know many authors who polished their writing as a result of their interaction with the other members of the group. They were not overly sensitive to the negative comments and were able to sort out the good advice from the bad. Both professional writers and novices attend writing groups, sometimes in the same group. Most of the groups I know about are what are called "genre groups." They focus on a specific genre of fiction or nonfiction. It would be difficult to mix writers of very different types of books because a certain amount of expertise must be developed for each genre.

Determining the Right Group for You

When you join a writing group, you have two responsibilities: one to yourself and one to the group. You need to determine whether it is the right group for you and you need to understand what you must do to make the experience a positive one for the others in the group.

You may want to visit a few of them first to see how they are run and whether the other members of the group are using it to help their writing or just want a social club. The kind of group you would want to join depends on what you are looking for and what your goals are.

Some groups have a facilitator who merely keeps it orderly and makes sure that everyone has a chance to read what they have written. Others are led by professional writers who help guide the group and occasionally make helpful comments and suggestions. My idea of a good writing group is one that will encourage your growth as a writer. The members are good listeners and supportive of each other.

It can be very helpful to a fiction writer if other members ask questions about the story or the characters rather than give their opinions. If it is a nonfiction book, they can ask about processes or technical terms because that can indicate that something needs to be clarified. If the leader is a published writer and/or an English teacher, he or she may give members the benefit of his or her expertise, but only if it is understood by everyone that that is one of the purposes of the group. Writing groups should not be conducted like a class. They work best as gatherings of writers for support and mutual gain.

The Memoir Writing Group

Although a memoir writing group is similar in some ways to other writing groups, there are a few ways in which it is very different. The major one is that it is deeply personal. All writing groups can be therapeutic because writing itself is often therapeutic but a memoir group is a lot like a psychological support group. When we are writing about ourselves and those near and dear to us, we are exposing our emotions and often our secrets, and we feel vulnerable. Because the subject is always personal, any comments that are made by members after a reading must be nonjudgmental. A compassionate word, a nod of understanding, or a smile of agreement are often the only responses needed.

Several years ago I formed a memoir writing group of people fifty and older. I didn't want to lay down rules but I knew there were a few things we would all have to agree to if it were to work. They were (1) to bring something they had written to read every time they attended, (2) to read only memoirs and not any other kind of writing they were doing, (3) to commit to attending every meeting possible, and (4) not to criticize the writing of the other members or the way their ideas were expressed. I reiterated what my mother had said to me as I was growing up, "If you can't say anything nice, don't say anything at all."

We did not concentrate on writing principles, nor judge each other's writing. Our comments were on the stories alone and how they made us think or feel. We continued to meet monthly for the next few years and I attribute the longevity of the group to the fact that we all agreed on the rules and abided by them.

Not wanting to be treated any differently from any of the other members, I made it clear from the beginning that I was not there as an editor or writing coach but merely as one of the members of the group myself. I felt that the only way I'd ever write my memoirs was to be in a group dedicated to the process. I was the facilitator at the beginning and later other members of the group took turns as the facilitator. After a few years we didn't need a leader of any kind.

At first the group members changed; some stayed and some left and others came to take their place. After several months we found that we had eight people who attended regularly and always brought something autobiographical to read. At that point the group decided to close the membership. In a larger group there might not have been enough time for everyone to read. We also found it disruptive when new members attended and we were reluctant to tell our life stories to people we didn't know well. During those months we had revealed a great deal about our personal lives and had become comfortable with each other. The memoir group was therapeutic for all of us but an additional and unexpected benefit was that we all became better writers, too.

After we had been writing for about three years I realized that our group had produced some very interesting stories—poignant, heartwarming, and even funny. I asked each member to give me twenty pages of what they considered their best stories and told them I would publish a book of them. The intention wasn't to sell the book to the public but to have a collection of our stories in a book we could share with our family and friends. When the book, which we titled *Reflections: A Collection of Memories,* was printed we had a public book-signing to share our experience and sell copies to anyone who might want them. The sales from the book-signing event covered the printing costs.

I had sent out a news release to announce the book-signing to our local newspaper the *Ventura County Star* and to the *Los Angeles Times.* Both came out to take pictures and write articles about us. A producer of *ABC World News Tonight* saw the article in the *L.A. Times* and said he'd like to interview us. He and a camera operator came to a memoir group meeting and taped us for a segment on their show. He considered the book timely and newsworthy because there is a trend of older people writing their memoirs. When the show aired, the segment on us lasted only a couple of minutes or so, but it was a thrill for all of us.

The members of our memoir writing group became good friends and we often had a potluck dinner after our meetings just because we enjoyed being together. It was probably the most gratifying group I have ever belonged to. Even though the memoir group no longer meets we have remained friends and make it point to see each other from time to time. Three of the members are gone now and we all miss them greatly. Nick and Phyllis were both in their 90s when they passed away but they were just as sharp as most people are in their 50s. Frank, who died recently, had a lot of health problems but he never missed a meeting.

I believe writing keeps our brain young. It's forcing ourselves to think in different ways, to plot and plan, to put together ideas in a logical way and then express them so that others can understand what we want to say.

How to Find a Writing Group

Most towns and communities have writers' clubs and many of them form small writing groups, often called genre groups, where you can go and meet with other writers who are writing the same kind of book as you are. If you can't find a writers' club you could check with the local library or bookstore to see if they have any groups you could join. The members of genre groups can be helpful with information on writing guidelines for their specific field of interest and the more knowledgeable authors could give you feedback on your writing style as it applies to the genre.

Forming a Group and Setting Down Guidelines

If you can't find a writing group to join you could form your own, as I did. Clubs, associations, and churches often have members who enjoy writing. It's amazing how many people want to write a book. Put the word out to the members that you are forming a group for writers and see what happens. You could also put a notice in the local newspaper with your phone number to call for more information.

When you form a writing group it would be wise to lay down some guidelines from the beginning. Here are some to consider:

- Set a time limit for each member to read his/her work, say ten to twenty minutes.
- Set a limit on comments between readings.
- Do not allow negative criticism. Instead, ask questions about the work.
- Be supportive of the efforts of others.
- Find something positive to say or make no comment.
- Try to make it to each meeting.
- Always bring something you have written to read aloud to the group.
- Do not bring writing in a different genre. Stick to the one specified by the group.
- Do not engage in personal conversations during the meeting. Save them for before you get started or after the meeting has closed.
- Do not discuss the content of a member's writing to anyone outside of the group. What you say there must stay there.

Some groups have written rules or guidelines similar to the above that they ask each member to agree to and sign. Some require confidentiality or nondisclosure agreements to protect each author's work that they will be sharing with the group. Although ideas are not protected by copyright, the recorded expression of an idea is and, of course, in a writing group that is precisely what members are doing when they write their pieces and read their work aloud.

An excellent example of the Nondisclosure Agreement for Submitting Ideas is in Tad Crawford's book *Business and Legal Forms for Authors and Self-Publishers* (Allworth Press, 2015). You could modify it to apply to your writing group.

It's best to choose a particular genre for your writing group, but definitely have a separate group for fiction and nonfiction. You could break down the fiction category to Mystery, Science Fiction & Fantasy, Romance, Christian Fiction, Thrillers, Children's Books, or Historical Novels, to name a few. Nonfiction could be broken into genres, too, such as How-To, Self-Help, History, Travel, Biography, and Memoirs.

Being in a writing group is great if it helps you keep writing. And you'll be encouraged to write so that you have something to read to the group at each meeting. If you come away from each meeting inspired and raring to get back to your writing it can be very beneficial. But if you have a bad experience and get discouraged by hurtful criticism, it can be destructive. You may have to try several groups until you find one just right for you. But when you do, you are likely to find it gratifying, as I did. The members of my memoir writing group will be my friends for life.

CHAPTER FIVE

The Rules of Writing

The best authors are always the severest critics of their own works; they revise, correct, file, and polish them, till they think they have brought them to perfection.

➤ Earl of Chesterfield, 1751

No matter how much talent you have, no matter how great your story is, and no matter how intensely your desire to be published is, if you don't learn the rules of writing you have a very slim chance of success. That fact shouldn't discourage you, though. Because you can learn the craft. You can't learn to be talented. The following are some pointers that I believe will help you understand what it takes to put your book together skillfully. In this chapter I have included a number of quotes by successful authors, as a teaching tool. They all have important points to make and they have delivered them succinctly.

Think of your proposed book as a story. No matter what you are writing—a how-to or self-help book, an autobiography or a novel—you should have a story in mind: a beginning, a middle, and an end. There must be a basic concept, continuity, and logical transitions from one paragraph to the next and one chapter to the next.

If you have not yet decided exactly what your subject is, just start writing. Don't stop and edit the first two pages again and again before you go on. Keep going until your book idea comes into focus. Once it does, it could be helpful to prepare an outline. If it is nonfiction, write chapter headings and a paragraph or two about what you plan to cover in each chapter. If it is a novel, write *about* the story. Tell sequentially everything that is going to happen and put this information into a chapter outline. Keep advancing the storyline and keep it simple. At this point, write quickly, concentrating on the story, not on how you write it. Also write character sketches, describing all of the major ones in great detail. You may never use these descriptions in the book but you will understand your characters so well that you will know what they would and wouldn't do. If your plot is character driven, as most of them should be, your story will probably change from your original plan. Don't worry about this for now.

Write from the Heart

Whatever you are writing, write with passion. Whether it is a mystery novel or a how-to book you must be enthusiastic about your subject or you will have trouble making it interesting to a reader. If you write a book simply because you think that it will sell, the process itself will not be rewarding and you will probably end up with a dull book. And dull books usually don't sell very well. Thomas Carlyle said, "If a book come from the heart, it will contrive to reach other hearts; all art and authorcraft are of small amount to that."

In his book *On Writing Well,* William Zinsser states, "Ultimately the product that any writer has to sell is not the subject being written about, but who he or she is." Your zeal, integrity, and warmth will draw a reader into your book, not hard facts and cold statistics.

Sidney Sheldon advises, "Write out of a passion, a caring, a need. The rest will follow."

If You Would Write, Read

Read works that inspire you, excite you, enlighten, entertain, or surprise you—books that touch your feelings. Read books that are quoted often like the Bible, the works of Shakespeare, and John Donne. Read the classics, the current bestsellers, and any books that may be a lot like the one you are writing. In *The Writing Life,* author Annie Dillard said, "[The writer] is careful of what he reads, for that is what he will write."

Whenever I am editing a manuscript for a book, I go out and buy a book that is in some way similar to the one I am working on. I focus on current bestsellers because they indicate trends in reader tastes and interests. The book becomes my evening reading. I study it, noting how the author approached his subject, what he wrote on the first page, and how he presented it. If it is a how-to book, I notice how the chapters are organized and how the information is explained. If it is a novel, I look at how the author developed the story, what her characters are like, and how they are described. Then, when I go through my client's manuscript making my little notes with a red pen, I know that I am not depending on training and instinct alone. I have a better understanding of what needs to be fixed and why, because I have seen examples of good writing in books that are currently selling in that genre. That is an added value that I never charge for because it contributes to my education as well.

With every book I read, I learn something new. I also learn a great deal about my own writing through editing other writers. It's so much easier to see other people's mistakes. We get used to our own and either don't recognize them as mistakes or become protective of them.

Keep It Simple

Walt Whitman wrote, "The art of art, the glory of expression and the sunshine of the light of letters, is simplicity." Simplicity does not mean the lack of complexity. It doesn't mean "talking down" to the reader. It may mean using smaller and simpler vocabularies, though, because that helps make the message clearer and more focused. And what is your point in writing, to show off your enormous vocabulary or to get your ideas across?

In Stephen King's book *On Writing,* he says, "One of the really bad things you can do to your writing is to dress up the vocabulary, looking for long words because you're maybe a little bit ashamed of your short ones." In *The Art of Fiction,* John Gardner states, "A huge vocabulary is not always an advantage. Simple language can be more effective than complex language, which can lead to stiltedness or suggest dishonesty or faulty education."

To understand this concept I recommend reading Ernest Hemingway, Amy Tan, Mark Twain, Barbara Kingsolver, John Grisham, and Truman Capote, to name only a few. They all write prose that flows gracefully from the first word to the last. When I am reading for pleasure I don't want to encounter speed bumps. I don't like having to keep a dictionary by my side to look up words I don't know. In nonfiction I enjoy learning new words and am happy to take the time to absorb information and gain knowledge. But when I'm reading a novel I just want to have fun.

Replace multisyllabic words with words of one or two syllables. Break up long sentences. Turn them into two or three shorter ones. Greater clarity will be the result. Long words and complex sentences tend to be confusing and murky. Sentences that are difficult to read and understand will turn away a reader. Usually such sentences contain several thoughts and ideas and become too involved to be understood easily. Remember always that our goal is to write books people will enjoy reading. As Flannery O'Connor said, "You may write for the joy of it, but the act of writing is not complete in itself. It has its end in its audience."

Simplifying our writing is not just a modern concept. It is true that books are now competing with television whose shows are often only a half hour long, and even that half hour is riddled with commercial interruptions. It might be that people really don't have as long an attention span as they once did. But the idea of aspiring for clear, simple, and concise writing did not evolve as an outcropping of the TV era. This principle has been around for a very long time. In 1580 Michel Eyquem de Montaigne wrote, "I want to be seen here in my simple, natural, ordinary fashion, without straining or artifice; for it is myself that I portray. . . . I am myself the matter of my book." In the nineteenth century Leo Nikolaevich Tolstoy stated, "there is no greatness where there is not simplicity, goodness, and truth."

The most powerful writing is that which flows naturally, expressing the thoughts and feelings of the author in a clear, direct, and honest way. Get rid of the clutter in your writing as you would your old, outdated clothes. Clean out the closet of your mind and let the sunlight and fresh air in.

Adjectives, Adverbs, and Qualifiers

An adjective is any of a class of words used to modify a noun by limiting, qualifying, or specifying. It is distinguished by having comparative and superlative endings like *-ous, -er, -able,* or *-est.* To quote from *The Elements of Style,* "Write with nouns and verbs, not with adjectives and adverbs. The adjective hasn't been built that can pull a weak or inaccurate noun out of a tight place. . . it is nouns and verbs, not their assistants, that give good writing its toughness and color."

An adverb is distinguished by the ending *–ly* or by functioning as a modifier of verbs or clauses, adjectives or other adverbs or adverbial phrases, as *very, well, quickly.* Stephen King says, "I believe the road to hell is paved with adverbs, and I will shout it to the rooftops."

Consider these sentences:

"I've got a gun!" he roared threateningly.

"You can't make me," she snapped defiantly.

"Oh, please do that again," she gasped breathlessly.

None of those adverbs was necessary. Delete them and read the sentences again. See if you agree that they are actually stronger without those words. Since the dialogue itself indicates the emotion, you might also want to avoid using words like "roared," "snapped," and "gasped" because they don't add anything important. "Said" works just fine most of the time and it doesn't get in the way of your story.

Qualifiers are words like *rather, quite, very,* and *little.* Try to avoid using too many of them. Examples of this are: *He was a rather insolent child. She was very embarrassed. They were a quite attentive group of students. I was a little afraid to read the letter.* All of those statements would be stronger without the qualifiers.

When in Doubt, Take it Out!

One of the best secrets of good writing I ever learned was something I discovered by accident while I was editing a nonfiction book by a medical doctor. I kept coming across complicated sentences and couldn't figure out what the author meant. As he tried to explain them to me I realized that he had already stated the ideas earlier in his manuscript and in a clearer way. In his efforts to reiterate what he thought was important, he had made his work more confusing. I found that it wasn't a matter of rewriting the lines to make them understandable. We could take the sentence out entirely without losing anything. His points then became more discernible and the writing flowed more gracefully.

You can't write clearly unless you are sure about what you want to say. I applied my new rule of "when in doubt, take it out" to other clients' works—as well as to my own—and the results were amazing.

Strip your writing of words and phrases that serve no function or are redundant. "The art of the writer," Ralph Waldo Emerson said, "is to speak his fact and have done. Let the reader find that he cannot afford to omit any line of your writing, because you have omitted every word that he can spare."

Active versus Passive Voice

There are times to use the passive voice and times to use the active voice. But, generally, your writing will be more interesting if you use the active voice most of the time. Among the definitions of *passive* are:

> submissive; not reacting visibly to something that might be expected to produce manifestations of an emotion or feeling . . . of, pertaining to, or being a voice, verb form, or construction having a subject represented as undergoing the action expressed by the verb, as the sentence *The letter was written last week.*

The definition of *active* is:

> engaged in action or activity; characterized by energetic work, motion, etc. . . . of, pertaining to, or being a voice, verb form, or construction having a subject represented as performing or causing the action expressed by the verb, as the verb form *write* in *I write letters every day.*

Show, Don't Tell

What exactly is meant by showing when we are only using words, not pictures? Telling is narrating what is happening. Showing is done through action and dialogue.

Telling is: *He was cruel.*

Showing is: *He would enjoy pulling the wings off a butterfly.*

Telling is: *She was being seductive.*

Showing is: *She whispered, "I'll be alone tonight if you'd like to stop by."*

Telling is: *He was bored.*

Showing is: *He looked at his watch and said, "How soon are we leaving?"*

We make our words come to life when we show rather than tell. Many writers also have a tendency to over-explain what is going on. A manuscript I recently edited made one area of showing, not telling, clear to me. The author frequently interrupted the narration to tell what the characters were thinking. He believed it was important to explain their motivations and feelings. However, it broke the momentum of the exciting story he had written and it distracted me so much that I edited most of the "thinking" out, leaving in what they said and did.

When the author read my edited draft, he did not object to the cuts. As it was a mystery novel he was writing, getting rid of those digressions kept the story zipping along at a rapid pace and kept the reader involved. In this particular book, it wasn't important to know what the character was feeling. The author had defined the personalities of his characters very well as he introduced each one. After that it was, in fact, more interesting to speculate about the character's thoughts and motivations.

A character can show what he is thinking by what he says and what he does. Using words to describe actions rather than thoughts usually works better. Showing can also be done through dialogue very effectively.

Instead of writing, *John was startled when Marsha came up behind him*, you could explain what your characters did.

Marsha crept up quietly behind John and said, "Well, hello, stranger!"

John jumped as though he had been struck. "Who the hell let you in here?" he said.

You could say that a character was angry or hurt or amused but it's more visual if you describe what a character did to show those feelings. Try to visualize your novel as a movie.

Showing is writing more externally, more expressively. Telling is usually more internal, giving an account of the action rather than describing the action in detail. However, there are times when telling and using the passive voice move a story along best. Unless you are writing a script that will be interpreted by a director, you have to write more than action and dialogue to maintain cohesiveness in a story.

As writers, we are faced with choices and decisions with every word we write. However, when presented with a choice, I always try action first, dialogue second, and everything else after that.

Similes, Metaphors, and Analogies

A simile is a figure of speech in which two unlike things are explicitly compared as in "O, my Luve is like a red, red rose," or "the sun was like an luminescent orange," or "sly as a fox."

A metaphor is a figure of speech in which a term or phrase is applied to something to which it is not literally applicable in order to suggest a resemblance, as in "A mighty fortress is our God" or "the autumn of her life." A critic once waxed metaphoric when he called James Michener "as sincere as his shoes." If you choose to use metaphors, please don't mix them up. In other words, don't start out by calling the sun an orange and end up calling it a volley ball.

An analogy is a similarity between like features of two things, a comparison. It is usually followed by to, with, or between. An example would be "Do you see an analogy between our boss and Attila the Hun?"

We have all seen metaphors, similes, and analogies in novels and when they are done well, they are delightful. In the hands of a proficient and imaginative writer, they can add interest and make the narration more colorful. However, I have found during my years of editing books, that when authors try hard to write a fitting colorful metaphor, it often turns out inappropriate and appears strained. Metaphors, I believe, should be left to the masters. Otherwise, it's best not to write them. And even if they are handled brilliantly, they should be used sparingly or they will get in the way. Although they are useful devices, when you use too many of them they can become distracting. It's hard to tell a story well when you are concentrating more on clever expressions than on advancing the plot.

Clichés

A cliché is defined as a trite, stereotyped expression, such as *sadder but wiser, mad as a wet hen,* or *as strong as an ox.* It can also be a hackneyed plot, character development, use of form, or musical style. A cliché is anything that has become stale through overuse.

Lazy writers use clichés. Creative writers avoid them. If an expression comes easily, question it. In *A Dictionary of Modern English Usage* (1926) Francis George Fowler writes that when hackneyed phrases come into the writer's mind they should be viewed as danger signals. "He should take warning that when they suggest themselves it is because what he is writing is bad stuff, or it would not need such help; let him see to the substance of his cake instead of decorating with sugarplums."

There was a politician who was so wont to use clichés that he was frequently quoted even though (or maybe because) there was very little substance in what he had to say. Here are a few clichés that I found in one short speech he made:

"I think this thing is a *rush to judgment.*"

"We would not *sweep it under the rug.*"

"If you think you're going to win this on what public opinion polls say eighteen months out, *I beg to differ.*"

"He's going to be in for *a rude awakening.*"

Who is that cliché-addicted politician? I'm not going to say. When it turned out the man was not going to run for president after all, the newspaper journalists were disappointed—he was such a rich source of trite expressions.

Although it is rare, occasionally there is a place for clichés. Vladimir Nabakov, in talking about his book *Lolita,* said "In pornographic novels, action has to be limited to the copulation of clichés. Style, structure, imagery should never distract the reader from his tepid lust."

Sometimes clichés can be fun to use in dialogue. Many of them are colorful. Among my favorites are "nervous as a long-tailed cat in a room full of rocking chairs" and "busy as a one-armed paperhanger in a dust storm."

The caveat is: think carefully before you use a familiar phrase. Is there a reason for it? Does it fit so well that any other expression would not do? Does it define a character? If the answer to these questions is no, then try to express the same idea in an entirely new way.

Slang and Jargon

Unless it is dialogue peculiar to a character, or illustrates the era, or has a definite use in your particular work, do not use slang. Slang words and expressions are in a constant state of flux, slipping in and out of style in short spans of time. Therefore, using slang will date you or your book.

Hip, defined as "familiar with the latest ideas, styles, developments, etc.; up-to-date; with-it," was once *hep* as in *hep cat.* These words probably originated with musicians.

Neat, cool, hot, bitchin', bad, righteous, fly, and *dope* are all words that can mean very good-looking, exciting, sexy, or anything really terrific. *Phat,* a word that is used almost exclusively by teenagers, means roughly the same thing. Depending on which high-schooler I asked, I heard that it means *pretty, hot and tempting,* or something or someone extraordinarily appealing. *Extra large* means really *phat.*

A word that is acceptable in one culture may not be in another. Musicians may use one term while computer programmers use another to express the same idea. Slang will be different from one ethnic group and one region to another. Many of the slang expressions that have now become part of our language originated with avant-garde musicians of various eras, such as the pioneers of jazz, rock, and hip-hop. New language creators are often young people living in poor neighborhoods.

The use of profanity has changed, too. Swear words are used more widely than ever before by the general public. In many environments, such as the entertainment business, there are no longer any forbidden words. Anything goes. We hear a lot of swear words on the playground and in schools now, as children have incorporated them into their daily language. I don't wish to discuss the right or wrong of such a development but simply to call attention to the changing mores of language. But, morality aside, the over-use of profanity, like clichés, could show a lack of creativity.

While *slang* is associated with very informal idiomatic speech and is characterized by the use of vulgar vocabulary, *jargon* is often used by people in certain professions. Psychology has words that can't be found in most dictionaries. It is fine to use the jargon of your trade or profession when you are communicating with like-minded people but not okay to use them in a book you want to reach a general readership.

Recently I've seen the use of such terms as "the F word" and "the N word" in written texts. But everyone might not know that the F word they are referring to is *fuck* and the N word is *nigger*. In some cases the word must be spelled out, as in the sentence, "calling a person 'nigger' is an affront, it's racist and cruel." We have all heard those words, including small children and great grandmothers, so who are we protecting? Besides, words in and of themselves are not "bad." It is how they are used, who is saying them, and what is intended that can do harm. It is when the word is used to disparage a person that it is wrong. When a word is used as a racial slur, an insult, or in any way that is hurtful, it is ugly. Even the so-called nice words like "honey" or "dear" can become very different words depending on the voice inflection and the way they are used. For example, "My dear, dear aunt died and the bitch left me absolutely nothing." Or a guy with a gun saying, "Give me all your money, honey, or I'll blow your head off."

I have no problem with the word *fuck* other than it is used so often and in so many different ways that it doesn't really serve to describe anything very well any more. I have been known to utter the word myself when I've been very upset, but I've never used it around my mother or my aunts or church people or school children, or with anyone who might be upset by it. Not because I think it's a bad word but because they may think it is and it would be offensive to them. I almost never use the word anymore because it is so overused that it has lost all of its impact. People who use *fuck* as an all-purpose word simply have no imagination.

When I was a little girl my mother used to tell me, "Sticks and stones can break your bones but unkind words can't harm you." It's true that words are not things. If words were bullets most of us would be dead. Words can hurt a person's feelings, though. They can incite rage and they can kill love. So it's best to choose the words we use carefully and to be sensitive to the person who is listening to or reading them.

In a novel, the use of slang, profanity, jargon, and ethnic expressions can show the identity or nature of a character. They can add color and authenticity. In nonfiction writing, however, unless the book is about slang or profanity, it's usually best to avoid them.

Point of View

Should you write a novel in first person or third person? Many novels are written in first person as though the writer were writing about himself. In *Huckleberry Finn,* Mark Twain wrote in first person and in the dialect of a boy with a limited education. And he did it masterfully. Ernest Hemingway said that all modern American literature comes from that one book by Mark Twain. It might be tempting to try to follow his example but very few writers can do it well.

Writing in first person (I, me) is usually hard for first-time novelists to do—and it is limiting. It gives you only one point of view, that of the protagonist. Most books are written in third person (he, she, they,) because various points of view can be explored and it is easier to advance the story. It is often called the omniscient voice, meaning *knowing everything*. Some authors go back and forth between first and third person. Some even mix several voices, each telling the story in first person. But these devices are hard to master and can be confusing and awkward. An author who does this very well is Barbara Kingsolver. She identifies whose point of view it is by putting the character's name at the heading of the chapter.

Until you feel comfortable writing in first person or mixing up the voices and points of view of your characters, it might be better to stick to writing in third person.

Past Tense or Present Tense

It is usually best to write in past tense, telling the story as though it has already happened. Writing in present tense often seems pretentious and unnatural. It also creates some problems when you try to tell the story "as it happens." You can't foreshadow events to come and you lack the perspective of looking back.

When you are writing a synopsis of your story, however, you should use the present tense. It gives it immediacy.

There are as many different ways to write as there are writers. Still, if you're going to do a thing, do it well. Don't take the easy way out. In accepting the Nobel Prize, Ernest Hemingway said, "For a true writer each book should be a new beginning where he tries again for something that is beyond attainment."

CHAPTER SIX

Writing a Novel

Your characters must become as real to you as to your neighbors; if they are not real to you, it's damned sure that they will not be real to your readers.

➢ Tom Clancy

Whether you are writing a short story, a novella, or a novel, the principles are the same. Your story is about your characters and embellished by events. But you need to have a plot to get started and there has to be conflict or you don't have a story. As novelist Peter de Vries says, "Every novel should have a beginning, a muddle, and an end." (Yes, the word he uses is *muddle,* not middle.)

Graham Greene describes the novelist in his own unique way. "Every novelist has something in common with a spy; he watches, he overhears, he seeks motives and analyzes characters and in his attempt to serve literature he is unscrupulous."

Learning the principles of writing a novel can be helpful to the inexperienced novelist but to have these principles demonstrated, one needs to read great novels. As much, if not more, can be absorbed by reading well-written books as by learning the method.

Some say that there are a limited number of plots. According to Christopher Booker, author of *The 7 Basic Plots: Why We Tell Stories*, they are (1) Overcoming the Monster, (2) Rags to Riches, (3) The Quest, (4) Voyage and Return, (5) Comedy, (6) Tragedy, and (7) Rebirth. Others have stated that the seven plots are (1) person vs. nature, (2) person vs. person, (3) person vs. environment, (4) person vs. machines, (5) person vs. the supernatural, (6) person vs. self, and (7) person vs. religion. And some say that all stories are about love, death, adventure, family, justice, and/or adversity.

Ronald Tobias thought there were more than seven and he wrote a book titled *20 Master Plots and How to Build Them.* Way back in 1917 Georges Polti wrote *The 36 Dramatic Situations,* stating that there were only 36 emotions tied to 36 situations that might occur in a story or performance. If you want more information on any of the above, you can research them in the library or on the Internet. The details are too much to cover in one chapter. I mention them only because I think they are interesting concepts and may be beneficial to your writing. Or maybe not.

Plot and Story

A plot is a plan of action. Think of it as your chapter outline where you show how your book opens, you list the major events, and you explain how the story ends. A theme is the central idea of a work. That would be your title and a brief sentence telling what the book is about. A story is the narration of events or series of events arranged in their time sequence.

A good story makes the reader want to know what happens next. The story grows out of the characters because the reader also wants to know to whom these events happened. Place, proximity, and time are factors in the story. Where did it happen? What was the setting? In a city, in a village, on a farm? In a living room, in an alley, on a train? Who was involved? How many characters and how close to the action were they? When did it happen? In daylight? At night? A hundred years ago or recently? These are questions the reader needs to have answered.

As the storyteller, you must make your reader care about your characters so you have to paint their pictures, breathe life into them, and make them important to the story. In every story there has to be conflict. What seems to outsiders as the perfect marriage, never is. All close, meaningful relationships are rife with conflict because all of us are different in our wants, desires, needs, and goals. Show the conflict between all your major characters.

Even though it's always a good idea to have a plan to start out with, don't make the characters conform to it. Let the story serve the characters. Stephen King writes, "I distrust plot for two reasons: first, because our lives are largely plotless, even when you add in all our reasonable precautions and careful planning; and second, because I believe plotting and the spontaneity of real creation aren't compatible."

Although I would never disagree with such a master storyteller, I do believe that it helps to have a plan, that it's important to decide what kind of story you are telling, where you want to go with it, and what you hope to find at the end. It's comforting to have a map of some sort. Even if your plot is no better than a hand-drawn map to hidden treasure and you find out the treasure wasn't there.

At least it's something to get you moving toward your goal. If you find that your story doesn't work the way you visualized it, you might discover a new path that will take you to one that does.

Characters

You could think of your book as a jazz group where the story would be the song and the characters would be the musicians. All of the musicians are playing the same song and in the same key and in basically the same time signature. They play together and listen to one another. But instead of playing every note that is written on the score, they improvise. They invent as they go along. Keeping the melody in their heads, they create a new way of interpreting the song. All truly great artists—whether musicians, novelists, painters, sculptors, or whatever—put their heart, their soul, their agonies, and their ecstasies into their work. It is more than an intellectual exercise for them. It is an exhilarating way of expressing their very essence—of revealing and dealing with their deepest emotions.

As you tell your story, ask yourself constantly what each of your characters would do now. The plot will develop naturally and authentically as a result of the relationship between your characters. The story is what they do as opposed to what they *should* do. Their individual nature determines what happens. They influence each other's lives, just as jazz musicians influence each other's playing. The most boring characters are those who are always kind, just, trustworthy, patient, loving, and loyal. These sterling characters are unbelievable. We all have chinks in our armor, skeletons in our closet, and a boiling point.

You must know your characters, their mistakes in life, their addictions, neuroses, self-esteem or lack of it, what they love, who they love, and why. Your story sets up what is at stake for your major players and who or what is trying to take it away. You will need to establish the nature of the journey and what the destination is. Your characters will then decide which route they take, and what they do along the way will determine whether they ever reach their goals.

As the author, you choose the game—or song—your characters are playing and prepare a basic playing field on which they will perform. You can tell them the rules but your players will choose how or whether to play by them. Plot happens when a character is motivated to take some kind of action and another character or group of characters must respond to it. One incident leads to another, logically advancing the story.

Avoid excessive exposition. Do not tell what happened in the past before the story begins. Let that information come through what your characters say and do. Although flashbacks are generally frowned upon by book publishers (and by television and film directors, too) they can be a useful tool in giving the reader some back story. Flashbacks can help explain the character's emotional state. This can be done through what a character recalls of past events, either through what she says or what she thinks. As tempting as it is to use flashbacks to fill in some blanks, please use them sparingly. They usually interrupt the story.

As the storyteller, do as little explaining as possible. Let your characters handle that task through dialogue. Stay in the active voice most of the time, using the passive voice when it is more appropriate for moving the story along.

Before you begin writing your book, write what you know or think you know about each of your major characters. Know your protagonist (the main character, usually the hero) and your antagonist (a major character opposing the protagonist) well. What are they looking for? What or who is standing in the way of their getting it? What was their childhood like? How are they different from each other? What are their personalities like? Arrogant? Shy? Self-centered? Religious or sacrilegious? Noble or ignominious? Beware of making your protagonist too good or your antagonist too bad. Nothing is more boring than a gorgeous, saintly human being who never makes a mistake or says an unkind word. No reader will be able to identify with a person like that. Also be careful not to make your antagonist pure evil with no redeeming virtues. It is much more interesting to show a vicious hit man, for example, who never misses Sunday mass, or a corrupt politician who lovingly coaches his daughter's basketball team.

When you start writing your book, introduce and describe your protagonist early on. With each new character who enters your story, especially if he is to play a major role, tell the reader something about him.

Character Descriptions

The following are excerpts from books where the author did this very well.

> My eyes swept the tent, desperate to find Marlena . . .When I caught sight of her pink sequins, I nearly cried out in relief . . . She was on the opposite side, standing against the sidewall, calm as a summer day. Her sequins flashed like liquid diamonds, a shimmering beacon between the multicolored hides. She saw me, too, and held my gaze for what seemed like forever. She was cool, languid. Smiling even.
>
> ➢from *Water for Elephants,* a novel by Sara Gruen

Sara Gruen describes what Marlena is wearing, and that tells the reader that she is a performer in the circus, in good physical shape, and probably very attractive. The author reveals the character's personality by how she acts in the face of a chaotic event: *calm, cool, languid.*

> . . . He judged Jack McAuliffe—with his tinted aviator sunglasses, his unkempt Cossack moustache, his flaming-red hair slicked back and parted in

> the middle, the unfailing politeness that masked an affinity for violence—to be a cut above the usual cannon fodder sent out from Washington these days, and this despite the handicap of a Yale education. There was something almost comically Irish about him.
>
> ➢from *The Company: A Novel of the CIA* by Robert Littell

In just a few words, Robert Littell describes Jack McAuliffe's physical appearance; he also tells us that McAuliffe is a refined and well-educated (Ivy-League college) CIA operative as well as a violent man with something comical about him. You know that this is going to be an exciting story. How could it not be?

> "I should feel sorrier," Raymond Horgan says . . . His look has taken on a meditative cast. Raymond's thick features fixed in an aspect of solemnity, courage, and a trace of sorrow. . . . He has picked up weight and a perpetual grimness of expression which suggests he has finally reached that time of life when he now believes that many painful things will not improve.
>
> ➢from *Presumed Innocent,* a novel by Scott Turow

Scott Turow shows the mood of the character: his *solemnity, courage, and a trace of sorrow . . . a perpetual grimness of expression. . . .* He also describes his appearance, thus suggesting that Horgan is overweight and probably middle-aged or older.

> Rose Sommers dazzled him instantly, not so much for her beauty as for her self-assurance and good cheer . . . she was a woman with a sparkling expression who seemed always about to break into flirtatious laughter. When she did, a network of fine lines crinkled around her eyes. . . . He could not judge her age—he thought somewhere between twenty and thirty—but he imagined that in ten years she would look the same because she had good bones and a queenly bearing. She was wearing a peach-colored taffeta dress and no adornment but a simple pair of coral earrings.
>
> ➢from *Daughter of Fortune* by Isabel Allende

In Isabel Allende's description of Rose Sommers you can guess that an important relationship is likely to develop between Rose and the man who is watching her. As she is an interesting and attractive woman, you want to know what is going to happen next.

> Anselmo was a short and solid old man in a black peasant's smock and gray iron-stiff trousers and he wore rope-soled shoes. He was breathing heavily from the climb and his hand rested on one of the two heavy packs they had been carrying. . . . The young man [Robert Jordan], who was tall and thin, with sun-streaked fair hair, and a wind- and sun-burned face, who wore the sun-faded flannel shirt, a pair of peasant's trousers and rope-soled shoes, leaned over, put his arm through one of the leather pack straps and swung the heavy pack up onto his shoulders.
>
> ➢from *For Whom the Bell Tolls* by Ernest Hemingway

When Hemingway describes his characters, you get a feel for their age, physical fitness, economic circumstances, and struggles.

> On the path comes a woman with four girls in tow, all of them in shirtwaist dresses . . . watch how [the mother] leads them on, pale-eyed and deliberate. Her dark hair is tied in a ragged lace handkerchief, and her curved jawbone is lit with large, false-pearl earrings, as if these headlamps from another world might show the way.
>
> ➤from *The Poisonwood Bible* by Barbara Kingsolver

Barbara Kingsolver's character description shows a determined woman intent on caring for her children in challenging circumstances. She is also foreshadowing events to come.

In each author's character descriptions, you learn about more than how they look, how old they are, and what they are wearing. You learn something about their personality and their needs. You get a feel for what drives them and an idea of where the character and the story might be going.

These are examples of how great writers get vital information across about their characters in ways that make you want to know more about them. Good character descriptions aren't just about physical appearance and demeanor, they contain germs of personality, nuances of motivations, and a foreshadowing of what is to come.

Make sure your story is like life with its ups and downs. It should be dynamic, marked by continuous change, activity, or progress. Some of your days should be calm, warm, and sunny and others cold, gray, and rainy. You need full-moon nights and sun-darkening storms. You need drama certainly, but you need quiet moments, too.

Your story should have a climax and a few turning points of varying degrees. A climax is the point of high emotional intensity at which a story reaches its peak. You also need to pace your story. There need to be moments where the pace is slow as your characters are engaged in introspection or in getting to know each other. As the story progresses, quicken the pace. Accelerate the action as you approach climactic points, making your sentences simpler and shorter, easier to read and understand. Imagine a friendship turning into a torrid romance and culminating in making love. Think of a symphony orchestra playing Ravel's *Bolero*. If the whole piece were played at one level of volume, with no dynamics or change of pace, it would become dull and meaningless.

Anne Lamott, who also sees the analogy of writing to music, explains the climax as "that one major event, usually toward the end, that brings all the tunes you have been playing so far into one major chord, after which at least one of your players is profoundly changed." If your protagonist has not changed in a major way from the beginning to the end of your book, you have no story.

And at the end, who won? Who lost? What is the payoff? What is the grand finale? You may not know the answers now. You might not find out until your entire book has been written and all the characters have played their roles. And maybe that's as it should be.

CHAPTER SEVEN

Writing Nonfiction

Books of the true sort, not those things in boards that moderns mistake for books—what they club for in book clubs.

➤ Charles Lamb, 1829

Webster's New Universal Unabridged Dictionary defines nonfiction as "the branch of literature comprising works of narrative prose dealing with or offering opinions or conjectures upon facts and reality, including biography, history, and the essay (opposed to fiction and distinguished from poetry and drama)." Nonfiction should not deceive but, whenever possible and appropriate, it should entertain.

Nonfiction covers a wide array of genres. Genre is defined as "Type: class; an artistic category marked by a distinctive style, form, or content; a distinctive category of literary composition."

Nonfiction has also been defined as anything that *isn't fiction.* So it would appear that there are only two categories of writing: fiction and nonfiction. But actually there is a third category. It is called creative nonfiction. It is writing that is composed of facts but uses the same literary devices as fiction: setting, voice, and character development. Memoirs, personal essays, and literary journalism would be examples of creative nonfiction. It is more creative than standard nonfiction. Although it blurs the boundaries between literary art and nonfiction, it should remain grounded in fact.

The following is a partial list of genres, or subtypes, of nonfiction.

- Science
- Satire

- Drama
- Action and Adventure
- Romance
- Mystery
- Horror
- Self-help
- Guides
- Travel
- Religious
- Science
- History
- Anthologies
- Poetry
- Encyclopedias
- Dictionaries
- Comics
- Art
- Cookbooks
- Diaries
- Journals
- Prayer books
- Series
- Trilogies
- Biographies
- Autobiographies
- Fantasy

In writing a nonfiction book it is important to keep it interesting. A good storyteller can make trigonometry exciting. Thus, many of the points made in the previous chapter apply to nonfiction as well as to novels.

Nonfiction is the broadest category of written works. There are different ways you would write in each genre. Histories and biographies focus on stories; cookbooks contain mostly lists; how-to books explain processes and procedures.

Accuracy is essential in nonfiction. And, in my opinion, so is truth. I have known writers who want to make a true story more exciting by inventing incidents that never happened. I choose not to cross that line between fact and fiction. Sometimes you may have to bend time and place a little to shorten what might be an overlong or tedious story but I believe that, too, should be avoided whenever possible. Changing the time or place of an event should never be done when writing a history.

How do you make a nonfiction book entertaining? You avoid stilted language, for starters. If your book is for a general readership, you will want to avoid using words that are not familiar. You follow the same rules of good composition that you would if you were writing a novel. That includes avoiding long complicated sentences, repetitions, and redundancies.

Interviewing

If you were writing a contemporary biography or a true crime book, you probably would have to interview quite a few people. It can sometimes be difficult to get at the truth because different people will recall the same event differently. Just ask any police detective how accurate eyewitnesses are and how many of them agree on exactly what happened. That is why circumstantial evidence is often more dependable than the testimony of witnesses. How can you know who to believe? You can't. You can only interview as many knowledgeable people as possible, ask very specific questions, and record the answers you get. You must do as much fact-checking as you can. Then you have to make some tough decisions as to what to write and how to write it.

I have been both an interviewer and an interviewee. I am always a little tense when I am being interviewed because very often the interviewer does not get the facts straight or reports what I had told her in confidence. It is now embedded in my brain: never tell a reporter anything you don't want reported. Only rarely have interviewers sent me their report or article before it was published. But I think that is the courteous thing to do whenever you can and it gives your subject the opportunity to clear up any misunderstandings or misinterpretations before you publish.

Whenever possible, record your telephone or in-person interviews so that you won't have to rely on your hastily written—and possibly undecipherable—notes or your memory later. You *must* get the interviewees' permission to do this, however, especially if you are interviewing over the phone, because your subjects will not know you are recording every word they say unless you tell them. It's important to be ethical and stay within the law.

If you are writing a biography, how do you get people to tell you the interesting stuff? Here is an interview trick I learned by accident when I worked as researcher and writer for the TV show *This is Your Life* in the mid-1980s. I had to interview the people who were familiar with the person whose life story we were going to feature on the show. When I asked questions of the subject's family, friends, teachers, and so forth, they always wanted to portray the subject in the best light possible. "He was kind and polite to everyone." "She was an angel." Well, we all know that a person who never makes mistakes or does anything wrong makes for a drab, uninteresting story. I certainly wasn't trying to get any dirt on the subject, a noted scientist in this case, because the show was about celebrating a life, not trashing it. However, I wanted some interesting, funny, or unusual stories about the man. The TV show was designed to entertain, after all!

Most of the interviews were conducted on the phone. There were the usual questions I had to ask. Where was he born? What was he like as a child? How many children in the family? What were his interests, hobbies? You know, all the basic information. Once I had the facts, I concentrated on what made this person different from everyone else. When I spoke with his siblings, I asked things like What kind of brother was he? Did he tease you? What incidents from your childhood stand out? One day when I couldn't seem to get the subject's sister to tell me anything interesting about Bob, the man whose story we wanted to do, I sat silent for a long time trying to think of what more to ask. The woman on the other end of the line finally could stand the silence no longer. "Hello, are you still there?" she asked. I replied yes and then she proceeded to tell me the most amazing story about her brother. She had been reluctant to talk about the event because he had ditched school that day, something he did often but was able to keep from his mother, an overworked single parent.

She said that Bob and another boy had gone fishing in the river (on a school day) when they saw a little girl thrashing about in the middle of the river and calling for help. Forgetting that he had never learned to swim, Bob dog-paddled out to her. His friend tied a small tree branch to the end of a rope and threw it out to him. Bob was able to grab it with one hand while holding the struggling child's head above water with the other. His friend then pulled Bob and the little girl in to shore. Bob and the child were lying on the ground gasping for air when the girl's mother ran over, picked her up, and rushed her to the hospital.

When Bob came home soaking wet and shivering, his older sister made him tell her what had happened. The child's mother later tried to find the boy who had rescued her child to thank him but Bob didn't want to be found. He knew he'd get into trouble for skipping school. No one but Bob's friend and sister ever knew he had saved a child's life at great risk to his own and he had made them both promise never to tell.

With Bob's sister's help we were able to track down the girl, now grown and with a family of her own. The host of the show told the story, then paused, and a voice offstage said, "Bob, I never saw you again, but I want to thank you now." The girl walked onstage crying and laughing at the same time, then rushed into Bob's arms. That was the highlight of the show.

From then on I knew what to do when an interviewee was reticent. I simply stopped talking and waited. It always worked. People can't stand a long silence; they feel compelled to rush in and fill it. That's when I got my best material.

Organizing Your Material

If you haven't done so already, put your written interviews, your research notes, and all other material you have gathered in separate folders. Then begin putting the book together. This is where doing a book proposal first will be helpful. You will already have done a chapter by chapter outline and decided what your chapters will contain. If you haven't done that yet, that is your next step. Then, start writing. At this point don't be concerned with the art of writing; just get it all down on paper. You can go back later to embellish and fine-tune it.

CHAPTER EIGHT

Editing Your Work

The manuscript you submit should not contain any flaws that you can identify—it is up to the writer to do the work, rather than counting on some stranger in Manhattan to do it for him.

➤ Richard North Patterson, novelist

Whether you choose to self-publish or plan to look for a publisher, self-editing is essential. With competition stiffer and book publishers' profit margins smaller than ever, books needing extensive editing are often rejected. As many publishers don't have the staff they once had, their decision about whether to publish your book may depend on how much work needs to be done on it. When they find a book they like that has also been well edited, they are more likely to take it on.

You may end up publishing your book yourself. And many authors have done so successfully. Many writers hire professional editors to put the final polish on their manuscripts before they send them off to be turned into printed books or ebooks. But that can be costly so it's best to edit as much as you can yourself first. In addition to the obvious—incorrect spelling and grammar—here are some other things to look out for.

- Words repeated in a sentence
- Repetitions of all kinds: phrases, ideas, descriptions
- Long, complex sentences
- A string of short choppy sentences
- Inconsistencies in style and punctuation
- Inconsistencies in tense (past, present, future)

Stylebooks

It is essential that you have a stylebook and refer to it often. *The Elements of Style* is probably the most user-friendly of them all. It covers elementary rules of usage, principles of composition, form, and writing styles. It's a small book—the one that I have contains only 105 pages including the index—but there is an amazing amount of information and wisdom stuffed into this classic.

Another stylebook is *The Associated Press Stylebook and Libel Manual.* This book is mainly for journalists but it would be helpful to any writer. It contains over 5,000 entries explaining the AP's rules on grammar, spelling, punctuation, and usage. An added plus is that it includes advice on how writers can avoid libel and copyright infringement. The *AP Stylebook* is organized like a dictionary and it, too, is user-friendly.

However, if you are really serious about writing and publishing a book, there is one that stands out above all the rest. And that's *The Chicago Manual of Style.* It is the most comprehensive of them all and the most difficult to use.

You can buy the printed book or you can get it online. The publisher states "completely searchable and easy to use, *The Chicago Manual of Style Online* provides recommendations on editorial style and publishing practices for the digital age. Now offering the full contents of the 16th and 15th editions, it is the must-have reference for everyone who works with words." I agree wholeheartedly. If you want to be a professional author your book should be edited as thoroughly as possible.

The first edition of this reference book was published in 1906. The most recent (as of this writing) is the 16th Edition of the printed book, published in 2010, and containing 1,027 pages. The printed book is not inexpensive but you can get a discount by buying it online.

The *Manual* is considered by many to be essential for all writers, editors, proofreaders, copywriters, publishers, and anyone else who works with words. Although the publisher states that it's easier to use than ever before, it still takes some getting used to. Even though I use it frequently in my work, I find it hard to quickly locate just what I'm looking for. It can be frustrating until you become familiar with the way the book is laid out. The *Manual* contains a wealth of information on many subjects. In addition to word usage, abbreviations, titles, forms of address, punctuation, and all of those details, it also covers manuscript preparation, rights, and permissions, and many other subjects. Manners of writing and word usage change constantly so it's best to get the latest issue.

Styles Change

Since the advent of the computer, some typing styles have changed. One example is that instead of spacing twice after a period and before the next sentence, as we did when we typed on a typewriter, we now space only once. When we used a typewriter, there were no italics available so we underlined book titles. On a computer we can italicize them. On the typewriter we used the carriage return at the end of each line, but on the computer we use word wrap. The word processing program allows us to automatically go to the next line. It can even hyphenate words automatically when we select that feature.

Dictionaries

Always, always use a dictionary when you have any questions at all about the spelling or the meaning of a word. Many of us misspell or use words inaccurately without realizing it and the wrong word can change the meaning of a sentence drastically. Spell check on the computer is helpful but it doesn't contain as many words as a good desk dictionary.

Whichever dictionary you choose, use the same one throughout the editing of each manuscript so that you will be consistent. When two spellings of a word are given, use the first listed because it is the preferred spelling.

Accuracy

Leave nothing to chance. Check everything you have any doubts about. Is it one word, a hyphenated word, or two words? For instance, you would write "this is for your eyes only" but use a hyphen when you write "this is an eyes-only report." Both crows-nest and crows nest are acceptable depending on the usage, but crowsnest is not a word. Different dictionaries may have different spellings for the same word. Sometimes it takes a few years for a new word to settle down to one preferred spelling. Some words never seem to, such as email. Some dictionaries show three spellings of it: E-mail, e-mail, and email. Others show only one or two. At this point they are all considered correct. So make your choice and be consistent.

There are words that you may not find in any dictionary that's less than five or ten years old. If you can't find a dictionary that contains newly coined words, check several sources, such as newspapers, magazines, and computer manuals for these words. But even that may not help you. I've seen *website* spelled *web site* and *Web site*. *The Chicago Manual* spells it *website* so that's the way I spell it now. When in doubt choose one and stick to it throughout your manuscript. The main thing, again, is to be consistent.

Your computer's spell-check is helpful but has its limitations. Beware of errors it will not pick up, such as using *their* (possessive case of they) when it should be *there* (in or at that place) and *emigrate* (to leave a country to live elsewhere) when you mean *immigrate* (to enter a country to live there).

Commonly Misused Words

Here is a list of words that are frequently confused and misused. Some sound somewhat alike and a few sound exactly alike, which is one of the reasons they are misused. And we can't depend on our computer's spell-check. Among the errors it will not pick up are words that are spelled correctly but are used incorrectly.

absorb	take in; reduce the effect of; deal easily with; consume
adsorb	to gather a substance on a surface in a dissolved layer (chemistry)
accept	receive; answer affirmatively
except	leave out, exclude
acclamation	an expression of enthusiastic approval
acclimation	adaptation of an organism to its natural climatic environment
adapt	fit; adjust; alter or modify
adept	thoroughly proficient; an expert
adopt	take another's child as one's own; choose to follow; accept
adverse	unfavorable
averse	reluctant; opposed
advice	an opinion or recommendation
advise	give counsel to
affect	to influence: *The plan will affect the outcome.*
effect	a result; an influence: *His protest had no effect.*
aid	to help or assist
aide	an assistant
alley	narrow back street
ally	confederate
all ready	completely ready
already	previously; so soon
allusion	an indirect reference
illusion	an unreal or false impression
altar	a table or platform used in a church service
alter	to change

amend	make minor improvements; correct an error
emend	edit a text to remove errors and corruptions
ante-	before
anti-	against
appraise	determine the worth of
apprise	give notice of; inform; acquaint
ascent	the act or process of moving upward
assent	agreement as to a plan or proposal; consent
auger	a tool
augur	a prophet (noun); to prophesy (verb)
bail	money in exchange for release of a prisoner; remove water from a boat
bale	a large, bound package of material
baited	lured; enticed; placed bait on a hook
bated	lessened the force of; moderated; *with bated breath and whispering*
bazaar	a shop; a fair where merchandise is sold
bizarre	strikingly unconventional or far-fetched
beside	at the side of
besides	in addition to
bight	middle part of a rope; bend in the shore; bay or gulf
bite	cut or wound with the teeth
byte	adjacent bits processed by a computer as a unit
bloc	coalition of groups or nations with the same purpose
block	solid piece of hard material such as wood or stone; an obstruction
blond	light-colored hair or complexion; a person with fair hair or skin
blonde	a blond-haired woman
born	brought forth by birth
borne	past participle of the verb bear: to support
bough	tree branch
bow	to bend or yield

brake	reduce speed; a retarding device
break	separate; destroy; fracture
breach	a violation, as of a law, obligation, or promise
breech	the lower rear portion of a human trunk; buttocks
buy	purchase
by	next to, close to
bye-bye	var. of goodbye; used to express farewell
cache	a hiding place; a hidden store of goods
cash	currency or coins
callous	unfeeling, hard, indifferent, unsympathetic
callus	a hardened or thickened part of the skin
Calvary	site of Jesus's crucifixion
cavalry	mounted soldiers
cannon	a mounted gun
canon	ecclesiastical rule or law; a standard, criterion
canvas	closely woven, heavy cloth; a painting on canvas
canvass	to examine or seek opinions; analyze; explore
capital	money; a seat of government
capitol	legislature building
carat	the weight of precious stones, especially diamonds
caret	a writer's and a proofreader's mark
karat	the proportion of pure gold used with an alloy
caregiver	a person who cares for someone sick or disabled
caretaker	a person in charge of maintenance of building or estate
caster	a roller
castor	a bean and the oil derived from it
censer	a container in which incense is burned
censor	prohibit or restrict the use of something
censure	criticize harshly; reprove; condemn
cession	act of ceding
session	meeting

chafe	to rub
chaff	worthless matter
chord	musical tones
cord	thin rope
cite	to quote; refer to as an example; to commend
sight	vision; a view; mental perception
site	position; location; place
clamber	to climb with hands and feet; a difficult climb
clamor	loud shouting or noise; a protest; an appeal or demand
climactic	pertaining to or coming to a climax
climacteric	a period of decrease of reproductive capacity; any critical period
climatic	of or pertaining to climate
collaborate	to work together; to cooperate reasonably
corroborate	to attest the truth or accuracy of: confirm
compare	to liken; relate; examine similarities
contrast	examine differences
complacent	self-satisfied; calmly content
complaisant	eager to please; deferential
complement	something that completes
compliment	an expression of admiration; praise
compose	create or put together
comprise	to contain; to include all
confidant	a friend to whom secrets are confided (*fem.* confidante)
confident	having strong belief; sure; certain; self-assured
conscience	faculty for recognizing the difference between right and wrong
conscious	aware; capable of thought, will, or perception
consul	diplomat
council	assembly
counsel	advice; a lawyer
continual	intermittent; often repeated
continuous	uninterrupted in time

corporal	of the body
corporeal	material, tangible
councilor	member of a council
counselor	one who gives advice
credible	believable or worthy of belief
creditable	bringing credit or honor
criminalist	a forensic investigator
criminologist	one who studies crime
cue	a reminder; prompting; hint
queue	a waiting line of people or cars; a pigtail
deduce	infer; draw as a logical conclusion
deduct	subtract; take away from
defuse	to remove the fuse; to make less dangerous
diffuse	to pour out and spread; widely scattered
demur	take exception; object
demure	shy; modest; reserved; retiring
deprecate	express disapproval of; deplore
depreciate	diminish in value; disparage; belittle
desert	a dry, barren region; something deserved; to forsake, abandon
dessert	a usually sweet food served as the last course of a meal
dialectal	of a dialect
dialectic	of logical argumentation
disassemble	take to pieces
dissemble	talk or act hypocritically; disguise or conceal
disburse	pay out; spend
disperse	scatter; dissipate; spray
discomfit	to confuse, frustrate
discomfort	to make uncomfortable
discreet	circumspect, prudent
discrete	separate

dual	for two, double
duel	fight
elicit	to draw or bring out; educe; evoke
illicit	not legally permitted; unlicensed; unlawful
emigrate	to leave a country to live elsewhere
immigrate	to enter a country to live there
eminent	prominent; outstanding; distinguished; noteworthy
immanent	existing or remaining within; inherent; subjective
imminent	about to occur at any moment; impending
energize	give energy to
enervate	destroy the vigor of; weaken
ensure	guarantee
insure	protect against loss
equable	uniform
equitable	fair, just
exacerbate	intensify, inflame, worsen
exasperate	incense, anger, vex, irritate
exercise	physical, mental, or spiritual activity
exorcise	expel a supposed evil spirit from a person or place
farther	at or to a greater distance, degree, or extent
further	same as above. Further also means "moreover" and "additional"
ferment	agitation; unrest; excitement; organism that causes fermentation
foment	incite; provoke; inflame; instigate discord or rebellion
flair	skill, talent; aptitude
flare	a bright light, an outburst
flammable	combustible (technical use: often seen on a warning sign)
inflammable	combustible (often used figuratively: *inflammable emotions*)
flaunt	show off; display ostentatiously
flout	show contempt for; scoff at

flounder	move clumsily or jerkily; flop about
founder	bog down or become disabled
forbear	to refrain or abstain from; to forgo
forebear	ancestor; forefather; progenitor
forceful	powerful
forcible	done by force
forego	go before; to precede
forgo	give up; renounce
foreword	introduction in a book; a preface
forward	toward or to what is in front of
fort	a fortified place occupied by troops; an army post
forte	an activity in which one excels; in music: loudly, forcefully
fortuitous	happening by chance
fortunate	lucky
gaff	a metal hook fastened to a pole
gaffe	a faux pas
gage	a security or a pledge
gauge	a measuring device; the size of shotguns
gamble	to bet
gambol	to frolic
gamut	the whole series or range or scope of anything
gantlet	an ordeal, an attack from all sides (also *gauntlet*)
gauntlet	a glove; a challenge: *take up the gauntlet*
gibe	jeer or taunt
jibe	be in agreement or shift sails
gorilla	an ape
guerrilla	a member of a military force
gourmand	a person who likes food and tends to eat to excess
gourmet	a connoisseur of fine food and drink
grisly	gruesome
grizzly	grayish or flecked with gray; a grizzly bear

hail	acclaim; attract: *hail a cab*
hale	healthy, robust, vigorous
hangar	shed for airplanes
hanger	frame for hanging clothes
hoard	a stash (noun); to store away (verb)
horde	a wandering group or a swarm
hurdle	a barrier over which contestants must leap; problem; obstacle
hurtle	speed, race, rush, shoot
hyper-	excessive, above
hypo-	insufficient, under
idle	not in use; unemployed; inactive
idol	an object of worship; a false god; a person or thing blindly adored
idyll	a scene of rural simplicity; a narrative poem; carefree experience
illegible	impossible or hard to read
unreadable	not interesting; not worth reading
imply	indicate
infer	draw a conclusion
incredible	unbelievable
incredulous	skeptical
indiscreet	lacking prudence; revealing secrets
indiscrete	not divided into distinct parts
ingenious	brilliant, clever
ingenuous	simple, naive
inter-	between, among
intra-	within
its	belonging to *it*
it's	contraction for *it is*
lay	set down; place or put; past tense of *lie*
lie	rest in a horizontal position; recline

lead to conduct, guide, or escort; a heavy bluish-gray metal
led past tense of lead: *He led them along the path.*

lessen to cause to decrease; to belittle; to become less
lesson something to be learned; a class; a teaching

loath unwilling, reluctant, disinclined: *She was loath to go.*
loathe detest, abominate, hate: *They loathe each other.*

liable responsible; likely: *She's liable to bring a date.*
libel a defamatory statement

loose not tight or bound; to make loose
lose to experience loss

luxuriant abundant, lush
luxurious sumptuous

magnate a person of great influence
magnet a thing or person that attracts

main chief; principal
mane long hair on the neck of a horse, lion, etc.; a person's long hair
mien a person's look or bearing

manner a way of doing something; one's bearing or behavior
manor a landed estate; mansion

mantel facing of a fireplace; a shelf above
mantle a cloak; something that conceals

mall a large retail complex; a large area used as a public walk
maul a heavy hammer or club; to use roughly; to injure

miner one who mines
minor underage person

missal a book of prayers or devotions
missile an object or weapon for throwing or shooting

moral virtuous; concerned with principles of right and wrong; a lesson
morale a strong sense of enthusiasm; spirit, mood

naval	of the navy
navel	umbilicus
notable	worthy, impressive
notorious	widely known and ill-regarded, as *a notorious criminal*
ordinance	law; practice or custom; religious rite
ordnance	military weapons as a whole; heavy guns; artillery
palate	the roof of the mouth; taste
palette	an artist's paint board
pallet	bed, platform
peace	calmness; lack of hostility
piece	a part
peak	pinnacle, acme, zenith
peek	to look or glance quickly or furtively
pique	offend, sting, irritate, affront
pedal	a foot-operated lever
peddle	to carry from place to place to sell; to deal out or distribute
persecute	hound, afflict, torture, torment
prosecute	to institute legal proceedings against
perspective	vision, view
prospective	future
plain	simple
plane	airplane; to smooth
poor	needy, penniless, destitute, poverty-stricken
pore	to read with steady attention; a minute orifice as in the skin
pour	to send a liquid flowing or falling; to rain heavily
practicable	feasible
practical	suited to actual conditions; sensible
precede	to go before
proceed	to continue
prescribe	appoint; to order a medicine
proscribe	prohibit; banish or exile

principal	main, foremost; the person in charge
principle	a moral rule; a law
prophecy	a prediction of future events (noun)
prophesy	to speak as a prophet; to foretell future events (verb)
prostate	gland
prostrate	lying flat
quiet	still
quite	very
rack	framework; spread out; torture
wrack	damage or destruction
ravage	wreak great destruction or devastation
ravish	abduct, rape, or carry away with emotion
rebuff	a rejection; a repulse; a snub (noun); reject (verb)
rebuke	reprove sharply (verb); the act of rebuking (noun); a reproof
rebut	to argue to the contrary
regime	a system of government; a mode of rule
regimen	a regulated course, as of diet or exercise
regiment	a military unit of ground forces
rain	shower; to send or pour down
reign	the period a ruler is on the throne
rein	the leather strap for controlling a horse
reluctant	disinclined; unwilling to act
reticent	unwilling to speak
retch	to make efforts to vomit
wretch	an unfortunate or unhappy person
right	correct; proper; just; appropriate
rite	religious ceremony; a ceremonial act
role	a part
roll	to turn; a small bread
seasonable	appropriate to the season; timely
seasonal	depending on the season

shear	to clip
sheer	transparent; utter
stair	a step or a flight of steps
stare	a steady gaze; to look at intently
stationary	fixed
stationery	paper supplies
stanch	to stop the flow of blood or other liquid
staunch	constant, true, faithful, steadfast; *he is a staunch conservative*
taught	past tense of teach; *he taught me to sing*
taut	trim; tidy; neat; tightly drawn; tense; *she speaks in short, taut sentences*
temblor	a tremor; earthquake
trembler	a person or thing that trembles
than	used after comparative words such as other (conjunction)
then	at that time; immediately or soon afterward; next in order
their	possessive case of they
there	in or at that place
they're	contraction for they are
throe	upheaval, tumult, chaos, turmoil
throw	fling, launch, send
to	toward
too	also; excessive
two	number
tortuous	full of twists, turns, or bends; circuitous; devious
torturous	pertaining to torture or suffering, *They toil in the torturous heat.*
trooper	soldier or police officer
trouper	actor; dependable person
trustee	a person to whom is given the control of another's property
trusty	a prisoner given special privileges for good behavior

vain	egotistical, proud, arrogant; fruitless; trivial
vane	a blade in a wheel to be moved by air, steam, or water
vein	blood vessel; a natural channel; tone; touch; thread
venal	corrupt
venial	pardonable
verses	stanzas; poems or pieces of poetry
versus	against; as compared to; in contrast with
whose	possessive case of which or who
who's	contraction for *who is*
wreak	inflict punishment; express anger; vent
wreck	destroy; tear down; the remains of something ruined
reek	to give off a strong odor
wright	one who constructs something; *playwright*
write	form letters on a surface; compose; *screenwriter*
your	belonging to you
you're	contraction for *you are*

The above contains a few of the listings from my book, *Abused, Confused & Misused Words: A Writer's Guide to Usage, Spelling, Grammar, and Sentence Structure,* 2013, Skyhorse Publishing. The book addresses the ever-changing nature of words and their meanings. In addition to the misused words, it lists frequently misspelled words and word roots.

Be careful in using qualifying or quantifying adjectives or adverbs with words that are absolutes. An example of this kind of misuse that is frequently seen is *very unique*. *Unique* is an absolute, like perfect, complete, equal, demolish, destroy, dead, and pregnant. *Unique* means existing as the only one or as the sole example. *Perfect* describes an absolute condition that cannot exist in degrees. It is incorrect to say *most perfect. Demolish* and *destroy* mean to end the existence of. It would be redundant to say *totally demolished* or *completely destroyed.* And we all know that you can't be a *little pregnant* or a *little dead.* There can't be a little or a lot of an absolute. It either is or it isn't; you either are or you aren't.

Other words frequently misused are *that* when it should be *who* as in "Is she the woman that sold you the hat?" instead of "Is she the woman *who* sold you the hat?" A person is a who. A thing is a that.

Was is sometimes used in the subjunctive mood when the appropriate word is *were*. Subjunctive is a grammatical mood typically used for doubtful or hypothetical statements. For example, I would say *when I was young* because I was young once. And I would say *if I were young* because I'm not young anymore and never will be again.

The word "whom" has gone almost completely out of style. And good riddance. Most people use it incorrectly anyway. The following is from Random House *Webster's College Dictionary:*

> By the strict rules of grammar, "who" is the correct form for the subject of a sentence or clause (Who said that? The guard who let us in checked our badges), and "whom" is used for the object of a verb or preposition (Whom did you ask? To whom are we obliged for this assistance?). These distinctions are observed less and less in current English. The usage cited above is characteristic of formal editing and is generally followed in edited prose. In natural informal speech, however, "whom" is quite rare. "Whom" still prevails as the object of a preposition when the preposition immediately precedes (all patients with whom you have had contact), but this juxtaposition tends to be avoided in both speech and writing, esp. in questions (Who is this gift from?) and sometimes by omission of the pronoun altogether (all patients you have had contact with).

Redundancies

It seems that so much writing is rife with redundancies these days. The most common one I see is "reason why." Say "It is the reason I told you that" or "It is why I told you that" instead of "It is the reason why I told you that." You don't need both words.

Avoid tautologizing as much as you can. Tautology is the needless repetition of an idea in different words, as in "widow woman." There is no such thing as a "widow man." Good writing is taut (tidy, neat, trim), not redundant.

Here's a list of redundancies that appear often, not only in everyday conversation and in writer's manuscripts, but in newspapers, magazines, and even on television newscasts.

absolutely certain
actual fact
added bonus
just exactly
radiate out
raise up
revert back
regular routine
resume again
reiterate again
right-hand side

left-hand side
alternative choice
may possibly be
meet together
minute detail
same identical
separate out
and also
completely full
sum total
deadly killer
drop down
rise up
fatal suicide
enter into
time when
protrude out
previous history
forward progress
baby kitten
annual birthday
follow behind
cash money

Omit Words You Don't Need

To quote *The Elements of Style,* "A sentence should contain no unnecessary words, a paragraph no unnecessary sentences, for the same reason that a drawing should have no unnecessary lines and a machine no unnecessary parts." Instead of saying *due to the fact that*, you could just say *because*. Instead of *in order to*, simply say *to.*

Consistency

Once you decide on a style, stick with it. Style is defined as the rules of uniformity in punctuation, capitalization, spelling, word division, and other details of expression. They often vary according to custom. Textbook publishers require a different style than publishers of romance novels, for example.

There are stylebooks for various kinds of writing. The one that authors of books use is *The Chicago Manual of Style.* Journalists would use *The Associated Press Stylebook and Libel Manual* as a guide to the style most frequently used in newspapers and magazines. Writers of manuscripts for anthropological and psychological journals, as well as doctoral dissertations would use the *Publication Manual of the American Psychological Association.* Knowing the styles to be used and conforming to them will help you appear to be experienced in that field of writing.

When you are writing nonfiction, don't move back and forth between formal and informal speech. The voice of your characters should also be consistent. If you are writing a novel and you give your character a certain pattern of speech, stay with it throughout the book. If he would normally say "I ain't done nothin," don't have him sometimes say "I haven't done anything."

Repetition

Once you have stated a character's title, described how she looks or what he does, don't do it again unless you have a good reason. If you feel that it's important to remind the reader who this person is, say it differently, put a new twist on it.

Some writers have a tendency to begin a lot of sentences with the same phrase. Often they will repeat a word in a sentence or in the same paragraph. This is called the "echo effect" by some editors. An example is *She was a beautiful girl wearing a beautiful blue dress.* We all have words that we use often without conscious awareness. To find those, use the edit feature on your computer and click on "Find." Type the word you suspect you have overused in the box next to the message "Find what" then keep clicking on "Find next" and search your manuscript for it, counting the times it is used. Here and there change it to a different word with the same meaning. This is where a good thesaurus comes in.

In writing a how-to book such as this one, some repetitions are necessary. There are issues touched upon in earlier chapters that need elaboration in others. For example, in the chapters on book proposals and query letters, I will be explaining some of the things mentioned before. I will give examples on applying principles discussed in previous chapters.

Flow, Continuity, and Transitions

In writing, *flow* means to proceed continuously, smoothly, or easily. *Continuity* is defined as a continuous or connected whole. A *transition* is a passage that links one scene or topic to another.

After you have done all the editing you can, read your entire manuscript through from start to finish at one sitting, if possible, keeping these guidelines in mind. Does it flow or are there words, phrases, or ideas that create snags along the way?

Do you keep going back and forth in time and, if so, is it really necessary? Maintaining a logical continuity helps the flow and makes it easier for the reader to follow.

When you begin a new sentence or paragraph, is it jarring, does it seem to skip a beat or to make too big a jump in the storyline? Is it too abrupt a change of subject? Good transitions can cure that problem.

William Zinsser advises, "Learn to alert the reader as soon as possible to any change in mood from the previous sentence. . . . Many of us were taught that no sentence should begin with 'but.' If that's what you learned, unlearn it—there's no stronger word at the start." I agree with him. You might have noticed that I start a lot of sentences in this book with *but* or *and*.

Transitions are also important when ending one chapter and starting another. Here's an example from *Island* by Aldous Huxley. At the end of Chapter 14, a character named Susila is speaking:

> "The moksha-medicine can take you to heaven; but it can also take you to hell. And then beyond the beyond, back to where you started from—back to here, back to New Rothamsted, back to business as usual. Only now, of course, business as usual is completely different."

That last sentence hooks the reader and signals that something is about to change. Chapter 15 begins like this:

> "One, two, three, four . . . the clock in the kitchen struck twelve. How irrelevantly, seeing that time had ceased to exist!"

Great writers know how to create page-turners. It would be hard to put *Island* down for the night after reading the last sentence of Chapter 14. Huxley was a gifted storyteller but he was also a craftsman. And craft is something we can all learn even if creativity isn't.

Being aware of the above principles and making the necessary adjustments along the way can help make your writing more readable, interesting, and professional looking.

Punctuation

How to use quotations within quotations and quotation marks with other punctuation marks can be confusing. But here are some generally accepted rules.

Double quotation marks are used in text to enclose quoted words, phrases, and sentences. Single quotation marks are used for quotations within quotations. And quotations within those single quotation marks should be double quotation marks again. Here's an example:

> "Alice," Mom explained, "your dad didn't say you could borrow the car, period. He said, 'Alice may use the car only if she comes to me and says, "I'm sorry I dented the fender and I promise to get it fixed" !' "

The ending punctuation is placed according to the person it belongs to. Mom is saying what Dad said he wanted to hear Alice say. As the exclamation point belongs to Dad's speech, it goes inside the single quotation mark. There should be no other punctuation marks at the end. Hopefully, you will never be called upon to write something that makes punctuation so complicated.

Commas and periods, in the American style, are almost always placed inside the closing quotation mark. In rare instances where it is likely that there could be some confusion, it may be placed after the quotation mark. In the British style, if they belong to the quoted material, they are placed inside the quotation mark. If they belong to the including sentence as a whole, they are placed after the quotation mark. In any event, if you always place the comma or period inside the quotation mark, you will be right far more often than you'll be wrong. *The Chicago Manual of Style* recommends the American style of periods and commas. Here is an example:

> Where once we called people from that part of the world "Orientals," we now refer to them as "Asians."

Use commas to separate the elements in a series of three or more. When a conjunction joins the last two elements, use a comma before the conjunction.

> Johnny, Suzie, Tom, and Jane attended his going-away party.

Most writers overuse the comma. Commas aren't necessary for clarity in a short sentence even when there is a prepositional phrase in the middle of it. But I see this often, especially when writers use grammar check. Not all of the suggestions in computer grammar programs are valid. Often these programs will suggest changes that are actually wrong for that particular usage. In general, use commas when they help to clarify the meaning. If the sentence can be read and understood without the commas, omit them. After all, a comma indicates a pause and a pause slows down the pace.

A semicolon should be placed outside quotation marks or parentheses, as in the following.

> William Faulkner once said, "Really, the writer doesn't want success" ; however, Faulkner certainly was successful.

There is rarely a reason to use a semicolon and it is a form of punctuation that seems to be going out of style. In most cases, a period and a new sentence will serve better. There are some instances when semicolons should be used for the sake of clarity, such as when items in a series involve internal punctuation.

> The children's ages were as follows: Sara, thirteen; Joshua, twelve; Jimmy, nine; Alice, three; Joey, two; and Julie, nine months.

Exclamation points and question marks are usually placed inside quotation marks. For example:

> Tina Turner's hit was "What's Love Got to Do with It?"

And from "Strange Fits of Passion" by William Wordsworth:

> What fond and wayward thoughts will slide
> Into a Lover's head!
> "O mercy!" to myself I cried,
> "If Lucy should be dead!"

Only rarely is the quotation mark placed before the ending punctuation, but you may see this and it isn't necessarily wrong:

> Who was called "the voice"?

Capitalization and Italicization

Names of places, regions, and localities should be capitalized: Middle East, East Coast, Great Plains, Golden Gate Bridge, Sunbelt. Also capitalize names of deities and sacred works: God, Jehovah, Allah, Zeus, Bible, Hebrew Scriptures, Koran.

Titles of articles, short stories, and poems should be capitalized and in quotation marks. The following should be italicized: books, plays, epic poems, magazines, newspapers, films, TV programs, major musical compositions, paintings, sculptures, foreign words and phrases, names of ships, aircraft, and space vehicles.

Make Your Writing Reader-Friendly

Be concise and clear not only through the punctuation you use but in the words you choose. Even if you are writing a scholarly work, it will be a lot more interesting if you don't try to use every five-syllable word you know. Do you want to show off your vocabulary or do you want to communicate an idea? Consider this sentence:

> Debilitating practices of procrastination, inappropriate decisions, and inconsistent productivity led to the administrative termination of the employee by the name of Oldham.

What did that mean and did you even care? It might be better to say "Oldham got fired because he put things off, made bad decisions, and wasn't always productive." Another thing wrong with the former sentence is that it is in the passive voice. The active voice is so much more interesting.

When you edit your work, see how many words you can take out. Fewer words, fewer syllables, and shorter sentences make better writing. That doesn't mean that your writing should consist entirely of short, choppy sentences. That's no good either. Vary the length of your sentences as well as your words.

There used to be a clear division between styles for writing and styles for speaking. That is no longer the case except in some forms of formal writing such as scientific papers and some academic works. But they could also gain by striving for simplicity and clarity over pedantry. Usually I edit manuscripts for books but occasionally I edit masters' theses and doctoral dissertations, and I edit those differently. In these academic papers, the jargon of the profession is used and it is not only acceptable but preferred by most institutions. Although the style for academic papers is vastly different from that used in books intended for general readership, the sentences still should be comprehensible and uncomplicated. Clarity is always in style.

Styles have changed so much in the past decade or so that many of the rules we once followed are no longer valid.

In checking what *The Chicago Manual of Style* had to say about split infinitives, I found this interesting footnote to Section 2.98, "Watching for errors and infelicities":

> The Press now regards the intelligent and discriminating use of the construction as a legitimate form of expression and nothing writers or editors need feel uneasy about. Indeed, it seems to us that in many cases clarity and naturalness of expression are best served by a judicious splitting of infinitives.

We can now split infinitives, end sentences in prepositions, and even dangle participles without being in error as long as we are clear.

Working with an Editor

Having someone with experience go over your work can be very beneficial. It's hard to be objective about your own writing and it's easy to overlook your own errors. Even though I am an editor, I need editing. My work is always improved after a professional book editor has been through it.

If you decide to hire an editor, make sure that you get someone who is qualified. Find out if the editor has worked on books before. You may want to talk to authors who have worked with an editor on their books or get references from agents or publishers.

If you can't find someone with experience in editing books, an English teacher or a published writer might be good choices. Be aware, though, that not all English teachers are creative writers and not all professional writers can edit.

Ask what the editor charges and whether she is willing to edit a few pages so that you can see what kind of work she does. Don't expect anyone to do that free of charge. Make arrangements to pay her for three or four hours of work. Then she can get an idea of how long it will take to edit your entire book and can give you an estimate of the total charge. She should also be able to give you some excellent feedback at that point so that you may do some corrections yourself before you go on.

An experienced editor will work with you in the manner that is most comfortable for you. If you want the notes written on your paper copy, she will do that, clearly noting what needs to be changed. I use red ink when I edit on the page so that it stands out. You can then choose to accept her suggestions or to disregard them. She will also be available on the phone for quick questions and clarifications. With most of my author clients now I make the changes directly on the computer, usually indicating what I changed. I have found, though, with many authors I can just change the manuscript and ask the author to read it over, checking it against his original. That is the quickest way to go because the author doesn't have to type the changes into his draft. If he approves of my edits, he can save time by using the manuscript I edited.

While working with an editor, you will learn by asking why she changed the items she did. Always feel free to question. If an editor resents that, get yourself a new editor. You are the boss. As I tell my author clients, "It is your book and it is your money. If an edit I made doesn't work for you, feel free to change it back to the way you wrote it." In some cases, the changes an editor makes is simply a matter of opinion.

When I find errors that an author makes repeatedly, I ask him to go through his manuscript and make those corrections before he gives it back to me to edit. That can save me a lot of time and spare the author an expense. Sometimes it is punctuation errors, misspellings, or repetitions that the author can spot in his writing in the future if his editor calls his attention to it.

Getting an editor means you have to turn over your "baby" to someone who may not be as kind as you are to it. It's hard to keep our egos out of our writing. If you are arguing with the editor, any number of things may be going on. She may have overstepped her bounds and be making a lot of changes that don't work for you and your book. She may be too authoritarian.

On the other hand, you may be trying to hold onto every word, closing your mind to changes that will improve your work. Sometimes it could be that you are experiencing a personality conflict with the editor and she may not be the right one for you to work with. An editor should be clear, direct, and honest about how she thinks your work should be changed. However, there is no excuse for insensitivity or harsh, negative criticism. A good editor will make suggestions, not pronouncements.

The editor should not rewrite your book or change your voice. She should have the ability to guide you and help you organize your work. She should make grammatical, punctuation, and spelling corrections, and show you how you can improve the flow of your work.

How you relate to the editor will have an effect on the outcome of your manuscript. If you go into the relationship with the attitude that you want your book to be the best it can be, if you can remain open to the editor's suggestions and keep your ego out of the process, you will very likely end up with a better manuscript than the one you started out with.

Whether you are working with an editor you hire or one who works for your publisher, recognize the fact that the editor is there to make you look good. A professional editor wants to help your book become the best it can be. Having the opportunity to discuss with the editor the changes she has made, whether or not you agree with them, can make you see your work in a new light and move your writing forward in giant steps.

My own experience with editors has been very good. The ones who worked on my books knew what they were doing and the edits and suggestions they made were usually excellent. That's not to say that I agreed with everything they wanted to change. In some cases I didn't and we would discuss it. Sometimes I could convince the editor that there was a reason for something she objected to and she then left it unchanged. Sometimes the editor convinced me to take it out, and I did so willingly. I consider that a good collaboration. This is a case where two minds are truly better than one.

My work as a freelance editor has been rewarding. As I don't take on clients or manuscripts I don't care for or don't feel qualified to work with, I nearly always enjoy the process. I've always found writers to be remarkable people.

Through editing many different kinds of books and dissertations, I have learned so many things. I have read material that I never would have read otherwise and discovered worlds that are very different from my own. And, interestingly enough, I have become a better writer myself for having worked with so many talented authors.

CHAPTER NINE

Presentation of the Manuscript

Keep up appearances; there lies the test;
The world will give thee credit for the rest.
➤ Charles Churchill

The best presentation involves excellence in appearance and attitude. Whether it is a query letter, a book proposal, a synopsis, a treatment, or your entire manuscript, it should be of high quality and presented in a professional manner. After all, your work is a part of you. It is one indication of who you are. Whenever you are speaking with an agent, publisher, or anyone in the publishing field, you need to present yourself as a professional, whether or not you have ever been paid for your writing.

As you are preparing your work, consider the following principles of presentation. The principles apply to many areas of life, but these guidelines are specifically for you and your written works.

The Professional Looking Manuscript

Think of your writing as your baby. Creating and birthing it isn't enough. As it matures, it needs nurturing and changing if it is to become the best it can be.

Average isn't good enough to get you published unless you are famous or already a bestselling author. Your book has to be different and/or better in some way than anything else out there to even get noticed.

Whether you are getting your manuscript and/or book proposal ready to send to an agent, a publisher, or a book doctor/editor, self-editing is an important part of your writing. The following are some things to look for.

Format

Although we are dealing primarily with manuscripts for books here, these principles apply to all kinds of writing. Present your work in the standard format for that genre.

For example: query letters should be single-spaced. Synopses for a proposed book are single-spaced. The other parts of the book proposal, the sample chapters and the pages of your manuscript, should be double-spaced.

A treatment (synopsis) for a TV or film script should be double-spaced, and it can be anywhere from three or four pages to thirty or forty, or even more.

There is a special format for television scripts for a half-hour taped series, a different script format for a TV "movie of the week" or a miniseries, and still a different format for theatrical film scripts. The script style for a stage play is different from all of the above. Generally, each page of a television or film script represents one minute of the taped or filmed show. A 120-page script, for example, corresponds roughly with a two-hour film or TV show.

Do your research, get samples of these formats if you can, and pattern your presentation according to the standards of the industry, genre, and entity to which you are making your presentation.

Appearance

Your appearance is the first impression you will make, the first thing anyone sees. If you were looking for a job you would want to be neat, clean, and appropriately dressed. Your written presentation needs to be all of these as well. Often the overall appearance of your manuscript will determine whether your work will be taken seriously. The more professional looking your work is, the more likely it will be read. Here are some pointers:

- Always send fresh copies of your work. Do not send copies that have been returned to you from other presentations if they have been damaged or look shopworn. No one wants to think that she was not the first choice or important enough to warrant a good, clean copy.

- Make generous margins. They should be at least one-inch on all sides. This is more inviting to the eye and easier to read. Narrow margins make it look like you tried to cram a lot of information into a small space. Framed with wider margins, the page itself is more appealing.
- The print should be sharp and dark enough to read easily. If you can, avoid using a typewriter. Inkjet or laser printers are best. Use a font or typeface that is easy to read. Times New Roman or some variation of it is good. And it should be in 12 point. Anything smaller is also hard to read.
- Edit and proofread your work several times. Check it for misspellings, grammatical errors, overly long sentences or paragraphs, misplaced punctuation and so forth.
- Don't send your work out the day you write it. Read it carefully again the next day or a week later to be sure that you are sending out your cleanest, clearest, and most interesting presentation.

Send Your Work to the Right Publisher

Publishers tell me that they get enormous amounts of misdirected proposals. Even if the presentation is professional, you don't have a chance if you are sending your work to a publisher who doesn't publish your kind of book. The same is true for literary agents. Many agents, like publishers, handle only specific genres of books. So choose carefully the person and company you send your query, book proposal, or manuscript to. Do your research to ascertain whether they are appropriate for what you have written. It will save the agent/publisher the time and trouble of dealing with an author who does not write what they represent/publish. It will also save you time, embarrassment, and money. When you figure in the cost of packaging, printing, and postage, it can cost a few dollars for each proposal you send out.

Then, when you do contact the agent or publisher, maintain a professional and courteous attitude. The tone of your query letter and of any interview should be upbeat and positive. Be yourself but be the best self you can be. Here are some suggestions.

- Maintain a professional relationship with the agent or publisher you are dealing with. Stick to the facts of your works, career, and professional experience. Don't discuss personal problems. Don't gossip or bad-mouth his competitor (who may have already turned you down). People in the book publishing industry often know, talk to, and even like each other.
- Be friendly and open, not overly formal. Relax and let your personality come through.

- Be courteous. Even if the person you wish to impress isn't, even if she doesn't recognize the fact that you have written the best novel of the twenty-first century, and even if he doesn't have time to discuss your manuscript in depth. If the agent or publisher does not want your book, that's no reason to be rude. You may wish to present something else to this person someday. It would be wise to leave a good impression.
- Don't apologize and don't be defensive. If there is something in your work or your presentation of it that requires an elaborate explanation or an apology, then it isn't ready to be sent out. Keep all negative comments out of your communications. Maintain a positive attitude and it will show through in all that you do.
- Project confidence. It's not a good idea to praise your own work highly—how can you be objective when you are so close to it—but you can exhibit self-assurance and present yourself and your work in the best possible light.
- If you get a face-to-face meeting with a publisher, dress for business. That means no bare feet or cut-off jeans, no micro-mini skirts or low-cut blouses (no matter how well-endowed you are), and no nose rings or green hair. Even though you are a writer and everyone knows that writers are eccentric, for this first meeting at least, be a little conservative in your appearance. Later, after your publisher has sold a million of your books, you can dress any way you like and he'll love you just the same.
- Be on time for your appointment whether it is for a telephone interview or a meeting in the agent's or publisher's office. If you are traveling to the meeting, leave yourself an extra half hour to get there. You never know what the traffic will be like. If you arrive more than fifteen minutes early, take a walk or stop at a café to have a cup of coffee or tea and go over in your mind what you want to say. But don't have an alcoholic beverage even though you may think it will relax you. The alcohol could be detected on your breath and even if it isn't, it's best not to take the edge off. That edge could help you in your presentation. You don't want to be too mellow.
- Be prepared. Bring an extra book proposal or manuscript with you just in case the one you sent was damaged or someone misplaced it and it can't be found. Anticipate questions the agent or publisher may ask. If you have obtained written permission to use certain material or quotes in your book, have it in your briefcase. Bring any photos, illustrations, charts, or graphs that were not included with your query letter, book proposal, or manuscript. Be prepared with names, addresses, and phone numbers of important sources, in case you are asked. Have a notepad and pen with you to take notes on what the agent or publisher says. Don't trust anything to memory.
- Show enthusiasm but don't be emotional. Don't threaten to slash your wrists or their tires if they turn down your manuscript. No cursing, crying, begging, whining, or complaining. Neither anger nor self-pity will get you a publishing contract.

Okay, you probably already knew how important appearances are and you didn't need those tips. But not all writers are as stable as you. When I worked as assistant to television producers, I saw all of the above presentations at one time or other. And, believe it or not, publishers have told me that people actually have threatened to kill themselves if they couldn't get a book contract, and worse, they've threatened to kill the publisher. There are some pretty nutty people out there.

Once a publisher has indicated an interest in your book, be patient. When he says he will call you, assume the possibility exists that he really will. Give him a little time to do so. A week or two at least. After that, if you haven't heard, it's not inappropriate to call his office and ask about the status of your project.

If you have been asked by the acquisitions editor to do more research or to get permissions or endorsements, you have a good reason to contact her again to tell her that you have done so. But don't call every day and don't always ask to speak to the editor personally. She may be very busy. Her assistant will probably know the answers to your questions and can give you the information you want.

One more thing: don't get discouraged if this time things didn't work out. If you got to speak to the agent or publisher directly, there must have been some interest there. Keep going. Keep sending out query letters and book proposals. Don't stop after three or four. It may take a dozen or a hundred contacts before you succeed.

CHAPTER TEN

Copyright Information

Take away from English authors their copyrights, and you would very soon take away from England her authors.

➢ Anthony Trollope, 1815–1882

A copyright is a form of protection to the authors of "original works of authorship" provided by the laws of the United States. It provides authors, music composers, and creators of artistic works the sole right to grant or refuse permission to use their copyrighted works. You do not have to register your works with the Copyright Office to secure copyright. It is secured automatically when your works are fixed in a copy that can be heard, read, or visually perceived either on paper or on a device. These would include manuscripts, books, sheet music, film, videotape, or microfilm. If your works have to do with sounds it is considered a "phonorecord." and your copyright is secured when your works are recorded on a cassette tape, CD, e-reader, or other device. The date that it is copied and/or recorded is considered the date it is created. It then immediately becomes the property of the author who created it. Although you are not required by law to use a copyright notice it is a good idea to do so because it informs the public that the work is protected. The notice should contain (1) the symbol ©, the abbreviation "Copr.," or the word "copyright," (2) the year of first publication, and (3) the name of the owner of the copyright. Example: © 2015 Jane Doe.

So, if you can do all of the above without paying a fee, why register your copyright with the U.S. Copyright Office? There are many reasons. A major one is that it establishes a public record of the copyright claim which must be done before an infringement suit may be filed in court. A timely registration will establish prima facie evidence of the validity of the copyright. Registration must generally occur prior to an infringement for the author to be eligible for statutory damages and attorney's fees (both of which are awarded in the court's discretion.) The owner of the copyright may record the registration with the U.S. Customs Service for protection against the importation of copies.

Violation of copyright can lead to serious civil and/or criminal penalties. There can be monetary damages of up to $150,000 per infringement for willfully copying or using copyrighted material. If a copyright owner finds it hard to prove the infringer amassed profits from the infringement, she can recover statutory damages of between $750 to $30,000. The penalties almost always exceed what it would have cost to license the works.

The History of Copyright Laws

Copyright law did not exist until the invention of the printing press in Europe in the fifteenth century. Before that it was expensive and very time-consuming to produce a book and few people knew how to read anyway.

By the middle of the sixteenth century, when books became cheaper and more widely available, the royal government of England granted a group of book publishers called the London Stationers' Company a monopoly on the printing of books. However, the purpose of this early form of copyright wasn't to protect author's and publisher's rights. It was to raise revenue and give the government control over the contents of the publications. And it was effective. The publishers, not wishing to risk the loss of their monopoly, published only materials that were approved by the royal authorities.

The first real copyright law, in the modern sense, was passed in England in 1710. Called the Statute of Anne (named for Queen Anne), it granted authors the exclusive right to have their books printed for a limited duration. After twenty-eight years, the works could pass into public domain. Similar laws were enacted in the eighteenth century in Denmark and France.

In 1790, the United States Congress adopted the nation's first copyright law. Congress made a major revision to it in the Copyright Act of 1909, reacting to new inventions such as photography and motion pictures. It was replaced by the Copyright Act of 1976 and, although the act has been amended often since then, this statute remains the legal basis for copyright protection in the United States.

Most nations have some form of copyright protection. The first international treaty was called the Berne Convention. It was adopted in Switzerland in 1886. Most of the countries in the world signed this treaty and they grant copyright protection to works of citizens of any member country. Although the Berne Convention is not actually an international copyright, it makes it easy for a creator to obtain copyright protection in other countries. The laws, however, are not always enforced and many countries violate the copyright protections. These violations have created a large market for counterfeit goods and unauthorized copies of books, music recordings, and videocassettes of films and television shows at very low prices.

Should You Register Your Copyright?

Yes. It offers you protections you can't get any other way. You may have heard that to prove authorship you can put your manuscript into a large manila envelope and send it to yourself. And when it arrives, don't open it, just file it away. That method of "protection" may cost less than a copyright registration but I advise against it and so do attorneys. Why take a risk when the cost to register your copyright officially is fairly nominal? If your manuscript has taken a year or two (or more) out of your life to write, doesn't it deserve the maximum legal protection you can give it?

The Advantages of Copyright Registration

There are some distinct advantages to registering your copyright with the Copyright Office.

- It establishes a public record of your copyright claim.
- Registration establishes *prima facie* evidence in court of the validity of the copyright.
- A timely registration will allow you (the copyright owner) to seek damages and attorney's fees. Otherwise, only actual damages and profits are available to the author.
- The registration may be filed with the U.S. Customs Service to provide protection from the importation of infringing copies.

Mailing yourself a copy of your manuscript will not give you any of those protections. The above information and a great deal more can be found in Circular 1, Copyright Basics, published by the U.S. Copyright Office.

What a Copyright Is

The Copyright Office describes a copyright as a form of protection provided by the law (title 17, U.S. Code) to authors of "original works of authorship" including literary, dramatic, musical, artistic, and certain other intellectual works. It is available both for published and unpublished works. Section 106 of the 1976 Copyright Act generally gives the owner of the copyright the exclusive right to do and to authorize others to do the following:

- Reproduce the copyrighted work in copies or phonorecords
- Prepare derivative works based upon the copyrighted work
- Distribute copies of it to the public by sale or other transfer of ownership, or by rental, lease, or lending
- Perform and/or display the copyrighted work publicly

It is illegal for anyone to violate any of the rights provided by the Copyright Office to the owner of copyright. These rights, however, are not unlimited in scope. One major limitation is the doctrine of "fair use." There are certain circumstances in which parts of a work may be quoted without having to obtain permission. For more about this, see the chapter on Ethics and Legal Concerns.

Another limitation takes the form of "compulsory license" and has to do with limited uses upon payment of royalties and compliance with statutory conditions. For more information on these issues, consult the copyright law.

Please be aware that when you register your claim to a copyright in a work with the U.S. Copyright Office, you are making a public record. All the information you provide on your copyright registration is available to the public and will be available on the Internet.

Recent Changes in Registration

You can now file a copyright registration through the Copyright Office (eCO) online system. The advantages are many. They include

- Lower filing fee of $35 for a basic claim
- Fastest processing time
- Online status tracking
- Secure payment by credit or debit card or electronic check
- The ability to upload certain categories of deposits directly into eCO as electronic files
- Available 24 hours a day (except for Sundays from 12 midnight to 6 A.M. Eastern Time)

Most online files receive a certificate of registration within six months of submission. The effective date of registration is the day the Copyright Office receives a complete submission in acceptable form. You don't have to wait for your certificate to arrive before you publish your book.

Registration with Paper Forms

Paper versions of Form TX, which is for literary works, are still available but it is the more expensive way to file. The registration fee using paper forms is now $85. The processing time is about eighteen months. You can download the paper Form TX from their website: www.copyright.gov. Fill out the form according to the instructions that come with them. Send the completed form, a copy of your manuscript, and a check for registration to

Library of Congress
Copyright Office
101 Independence Avenue, S.E.
Washington, DC 20559-6000

These fees were in effect as of May 1, 2014. As fees change every few years, be sure to check with the Copyright Office for updates. For more information and instructions on how to file your copyright by any of the above means, go to www.copyright.gov/register/.

When you use the Copyright Office's eCO System, you send your manuscript electronically. When you register using the paper forms you will be sending your application, check, and a printed manuscript by mail. The printed paper copy can be computer generated, typed on a typewriter, or handwritten. You may use any paper size. To facilitate handling and long-term storage it would be a good idea to staple, clip, or bind it in some way. This brings up another interesting provision of the copyright law called "mandatory deposit."

Mandatory Deposit Requirements

To quote directly from Circular 7d, "All works under copyright protection and published in the United States on or after March 1, 1989, are subject to mandatory deposit whether published with or without a notice [of copyright]. Section 704 of the Copyright Act states that these deposits 'are available to the Library of Congress for its collections, or for exchange or transfer to any other library.' Section 407 of the copyright law requires the 'owner of copyright or of the exclusive right of publication' in a work published in the United States to deposit the required number of copies in the Copyright Office within three months of the date of such publication."

You are required to send two copies of the best edition of your copyrightable work. Best edition is defined as the copy of the highest quality. For example, if you have loose manuscript pages of your book as well as a bound edition, your "best edition" is the one that is bound.

Publication is defined in the copyright law as "the distribution of copies or phonorecords of a work to the public by sale or other transfer of ownership, or by rental, lease, or lending."

Deposits should be sent to:
Library of Congress
Register of Copyrights
Attn: 407 Deposits
101 Independence Avenue, S.E.
Washington, DC 20559-6000

Again, since the rules are subject to change, always check with the Copyright Office for updates.

Registering Under a Pseudonym or Pen Name

You may use a pseudonym or pen name when registering your copyright, but the pseudonym itself is not protected by copyright. If you are writing under a pseudonym but want to be identified by your legal name in the copyright records, give your legal name followed by your pseudonym in space 2, "Name and Address of Author and Owner of the Copyright."

For example, Samuel Clemens would fill in space 2 as follows: "Samuel Langhorne Clemens whose pseudonym is Mark Twain."

Also check "yes" in the box next to "Pseudonymous?" at space 2. If you do not wish your identity revealed in the records, give your pseudonym and identify it as such.

Example: "Mark Twain, pseudonym."

You may also leave the space blank but you still must identify the citizenship or domicile of the author. You may use a pseudonym in space 4 but do not leave this space blank. However, be warned that if you hold your copyright under a fictitious name, you may have problems proving ownership in any business dealings. It's best to consult an attorney in this case.

What Cannot Be Copyrighted?

- Works that have not been fixed in a tangible form of expression, such as improvised speeches, dances, or music that has not been written or recorded

- Ideas, procedures, methods, systems, processes, concepts, principles, discoveries or devices, as distinguished from a description, explanation, or illustration
- Titles, names, short phrases and slogans, familiar symbols or designs, variations of lettering or coloring, lists of ingredients or contents
- Works consisting entirely of information that is common property and containing no original authorship, such as calendars, height and weight charts, tape measures and rulers, and lists or tables taken from public documents or other common sources

Copyrighting Recipes

A question that comes up often is: If a list of ingredients in a recipe can't be copyrighted, what protection does a cookbook author have? According to the Copyright office, when a recipe is "accompanied by substantial literary expression in the form of an explanation or directions, or when there is a combination of recipes, as in a cookbook, there may be a basis for copyright protection." Protection extends only to "original works of authorship" that are fixed in a tangible form. The author must have "produced the work by his own intellectual effort, as distinguished from copying an existing work."

So if you are writing a cookbook that contains original recipes and you want to register the copyright, be sure to include, along with the list of ingredients, your directions or instructions for preparing each of the recipes. For more information, get "Copyright Registration of Recipes," FL 122, from the Copyright Office.

Is a Notice of Copyright Required?

Under U.S. law a copyright notice is no longer required but it is still a good idea to indicate that your work is copyrighted. Use of the notice identifies the copyright owner and the first year of publication. If a proper notice of copyright appears on the published work, no one can claim they didn't know the work was protected.

The use of the copyright notice is your responsibility. You don't need permission from the Copyright Office to use it. And you do not have to register it first.

How to Reach the Copyright Office

For general information, you may call the Copyright Public Information Office at (202) 707-3000 between the hours of 8:30 a.m. and 5:00 p.m. Eastern time,

Monday through Friday. Their toll free number is 877-476-0778. Circulars, announcements, certain application forms, and other materials are available from the Copyright Office website at www.copyright.gov. To request paper application forms or circulars, call the Forms and Publications Hotline at 202/707-9100 and leave a recorded message.

For information by regular mail, write to:

Library of Congress

Copyright Office-COPUBS

101 Independence Avenue, S.E.

Washington, DC 20559-6304

There are four types of protection for your work: copyright registration, registration with the Writers Guild of America, trademarks, and patents. The following is a brief explanation of each one.

A copyright © is a form of intellectual property law. It protects original works of authorship including literary, dramatic, musical, and artistic works, such as poetry, novels, movies, songs, computer software, and architecture. Copyright does not protect facts, ideas, systems, or methods of operation, although it may protect the way these things are expressed.

If you have written a script or treatment for radio, television, film, video, or interactive media you can register it with the Writers Guild of America. It provides a dated record of your claim. For more information on registration go to their website, WGAWRegistry.org. The fee is $20.

A trademark™ protects words, phrases, symbols, or designs identifying the source of the goods or services of one party and distinguishing them from those of others. You aren't required to register your mark to establish claim over it. The registered mark® is used if you have filed an application with the U.S. Patent and Trademark Office (USPTO).

A patent is an intellectual property right granted to an inventor. It prevents others from making, using, or selling the invention throughout the United States or importing the invention into the United States. Patents last for a limited time and come in exchange for publically disclosing the invention with the patent. There are three types of patents you can apply for, based on the type of invention: utility, design, and plant (the kind that usually grows in soil).

For more information on patents and trademarks go to www.uspto.gov.

CHAPTER ELEVEN

Literary Agents

For many authors, an agent agreement is the first agreement they will ever face in their literary endeavors . . . it is critical to remember that the agent works for the author and not the reverse.

➢ National Writers Union

As in all professions, there are good agents and there are bad agents. And a bad agent is worse than none at all. Before you begin looking for representation, you should know a few facts so that you can determine whether having a literary agent will be in your best interests. The type of book you are writing and how it will be distributed may influence your decision. You may find that, in some cases, an agent is unnecessary and may only get in your way.

If you decide that you must have an agent, this chapter will provide you with information on finding the qualified agent who is best suited for you and your work.

Do You Need an Agent?

The answer to that question depends on several factors. If you plan to contact small publishers or if you already have access to publishers who may want to publish your book, you may not need an agent to help you get a contract. However, unless you are good at negotiating and understand the book publishing industry well, you may find that an agent will be able to get you a better deal than you can get for yourself.

Smaller houses will usually accept queries and book proposals from individual authors, and, in fact, some prefer to deal with an author who does not have an agent. But if you want to reach a major publisher such as Simon & Schuster or Random House you will probably need an established agent to represent you. Large publishing houses rarely deal directly with an author before the contract is signed.

If you choose not to have a literary agent represent you, it could be advantageous to have an attorney who specializes in intellectual property and/or entertainment law to look over any publishing contract that is offered you. You may want to do that even if you do have an agent because the contract may be complex and beyond the area of expertise of an agent. Although you would have to pay a lawyer a fee, you wouldn't have to share your royalties with an attorney as you would with an agent. However, many lawyers won't review book contracts unless the dollar amounts are large.

One of the benefits of membership in the National Writers Union and the Authors Guild is free contract advice for writers dealing with an agent or publisher. In addition to advice, the National Writers Union provides members with the NWU Preferred Literary Agent Agreement and the Authors Guild provides the Guild's Model Trade Book Contract. See the chapter on literary organizations for more information.

The decision to retain an agent is a major one in your career. It is important for you to know as much as you can about the agent you choose and to understand the agency agreement. Even if you have an agent, you should participate in all the decisions that affect your life as an author and educate yourself at every level of your career. Knowledge is power.

The big monetary advances that publishers have given authors in the past are a thing of the past except in rare cases. The new reality is that even major publishers do not offer large advances anymore unless you are a famous person or a proven author who regularly sells books in the thousands or hundreds of thousands.

Since the smaller publishers often do not give authors any advance, an agent is reluctant to represent an author who will appeal only to small publishers. Fifteen percent of nothing is still nothing. The agent won't realize any financial remuneration until your royalties start to roll in—and that could take years.

There are clear advantages and disadvantages to having a literary agent.

The Advantages

Qualified agents have access to major publishers and are more likely to get you an offer than you are yourself. After all, that is their specialty. They will probably get you a larger advance and bigger royalties than you could negotiate for, as well as a more advantageous contract all around. Experienced agents know what to watch for in a publishing contract and how to protect your rights. Jonathan Kirsch, an attorney specializing in intellectual property matters and publishing law, and author of *Kirsch's Guide to the Book Contract,* advises:

> An experienced agent will be far more adept, insightful, and effective in dealing with the legal technicalities of a book contract than an attorney who lacks long and specific experience in the book publishing industry.
>
> An established agent will know which publishers buy the kind of book you are writing. They may already have a relationship with particular publishers through placing other books with them. Good agents may also nurture new authors and help guide their careers.

The Disadvantages

One obvious disadvantage is that you will probably be required to give the agent 15 percent of your advance and royalties. For example, if she negotiates an advance of $5,000, you will receive $4,250 and she will get $750. The money won't come directly to you. The check is mailed to your agent who takes her percentage out and then sends you a check for the remaining amount. The same is true for your royalty checks, which are usually paid twice a year.

Once you have signed with an agent, you may not be able to make a deal with publishers on your own. So even though you may have contacts within a particular publishing company, you may have trouble working with them without first getting the approval of your agent. If you have signed an agreement with the agent for representation for a period of two years and the agent does nothing for you, it may be complicated for you to get out of that relationship.

Some literary agents specialize in representing authors of books and may not have any connections with the television or film industry. If they don't have experience analyzing and negotiating TV and film deals, you may need a separate agent for that. If you have written a script or a treatment (synopsis) for a proposed film or television production it would be better for you to find an agent who deals mainly with that industry and is signatory to the Writers Guild of America (WGA). WGA agents are required to charge no more than 10 percent.

You might also want to consider registering your script with the Writers Guild. It establishes a dated record of your authorship and provides protection in addition to your copyright registration. Go to WGAWRegistry.org for more information.

How Do Agents Get New Clients?

There are several ways agents get clients. These are the major ones, in order of frequency and likelihood.

- Through referrals. These may come from existing clients, editors, other agents, published authors, or experts in a particular field
- Through their speaking engagements at writers conferences and seminars
- Through written queries from authors

If you have met an agent through a seminar, writers conference, business associate, or some other way in which you have made personal contact, it is not inappropriate to call and ask if you may send a query letter. If the agent is not too busy, you may even have the opportunity to pitch your idea over the phone.

How Do You Find an Agent?

To look for an agent, check *Literary Market Place* published by R.R. Bowker, *Guide to Literary Agents* published by Writer's Digest Books, or *The Insider's Guide to Book Editors, Publishers & Literary Agents* by Jeff Herman, published by Prima Communications. *Writer's Market* and *The Writer's Handbook* now list agents but the listings are not extensive. Occasionally, writer magazines such as *Writer's Digest, The Writer,* and *Poets and Writers* will have articles mentioning agents who are open to new writers.

An agent is not necessarily qualified just because he is listed in the above guides. Some of them may be "business card" agents and may not be experienced or reputable. Literary agents are not like an attorney or building contractor. They don't have to pass exams, adhere to any rules, or prove their level of competence. They don't need a license from any regulatory agency. They can simply print up business cards and call themselves literary agents. Their listing, though, is a starting point in your search for someone to represent you because it will tell you what kinds of books they work with.

Get the latest issue of the guides and periodicals because agents move, go out of business, or are otherwise not available from year to year. Some of the above have websites and you may be able to do much of your research over the Internet.

Like publishers, many agents specialize in a particular genre such as how-to, spirituality, health, mysteries, children's books, historical fiction, biography, and so forth. Because nonfiction books are easier to sell than novels, especially by first-time authors, most agents represent nonfiction writers. If you are a novelist, you may have a tougher time finding a literary agent. The closer you can match the agent to the type of book you are writing, the better chance you will have that he will be interested in representing you and your book.

Before you contact any agents, notice whether they want to be queried first or will accept a synopsis or a book proposal along with your query or cover letter. Very few will want to look at a complete manuscript on first contact.

How Do You Choose the Right Agent?

Whenever possible, get recommendations from authors, publishers, editors, or others who have dealt with the agent.

An agent may suggest that your manuscript would have a better chance of being accepted by a publisher if you have it edited. That may be a valid comment as most manuscripts do need professional editing. But beware if the agent refers you to a specific company. Some agents receive referral fees from editing companies and may be more interested in collecting their fee than in helping you. Those agents may not agree to represent you even after your book has been edited by someone they recommended. You could spend a lot of money on an editor who is not right for your book and still end up without an agent.

For information on qualified agents, check with the Association of Authors' Representatives and the National Writers Union who require literary agents to be qualified and to abide by a high standard of ethics to be listed with them. The Writers Guild of America also requires the agent to prove their experience and qualifications in order to be a signatory to their organization.

What to Watch Out For

Some agents charge a reading fee of up to $450. As that may be a major source of income for them rather than a percentage of your advance and royalties, they may not be operating in your best interests.

Although the AAR does not accept agents who charge reading fees, there are a few fee-charging agents who are legitimate and render a valuable service to writers. But picking a good one out of the crowd is hard to do. If an agent merely reads your manuscript and then passes on it you will have learned nothing. Some agents will send a report and then ask for an additional fee for a more detailed analysis. That practice is highly suspect. If you think you have found a responsible, ethical fee-charging agent and decide to send your material to her, be sure that you will get something in return. Ask the following questions:

- What services do you provide for the reading fee?
- Will my material be evaluated by someone with professional experience?

- Will I receive a detailed report with editorial suggestions and the book's marketability?
- How long before I receive a report?
- What is the fee for a complete analysis?
- If you decide to accept me as a client will the fee be refunded?

Don't be afraid to ask for information from the agent about his charges, method of working, and experience as well as a list of his clients' published books. Remember, the agent is paid by you, not the other way around. You have a right to know everything about him that will help you in your selection.

It is important to choose an agent who is not only ethical and experienced but is someone you feel rapport with. The National Writers Union gets many complaints from writers who have been defrauded and mistreated by agents. Many so-called agents are nothing but scam artists.

Script agents are in a different category from literary agents. Those who are signatory to the Writers Guild of America cannot charge more than a 10 percent commission and they must abide by a standard code of behavior.

Although it will be helpful to get a list of approved agents from the Association of Authors' Representatives, there are other organizations as well that can give you valuable information on specific agents. The National Writers Union maintains an Agent Database available to NWU members. Many working writers join the NWU because of the benefits and protections they offer. The Agent Research & Evaluation Company tracks agents in court records and the press. They've been around since 1980 and have a good reputation. They sell reports from their database and you can get a summary on an agent from them. The Fisher Report publishes a list of disreputable agents. The American Society of Journalists and Authors reports problems with agents from time to time in their Contract Watch. The above, along with contact information, are listed in Resources in the back of this book.

Once you have decided on which agents to query—and you may want to choose several—you can begin to compose your letter, customizing it to fit each particular agent. (See chapter on Query Letters.)

CHAPTER TWELVE

The Book Proposal

A good book is the precious life-blood of a master spirit, embalmed and treasured up on purpose to a life beyond life.

➤ John Milton

As great a book as yours might be, you can't expect it to reach readers without a great deal of help. Your choices are to self-publish your book and figure out how to promote, sell, and distribute it yourself, or to find a publisher for it who will do all that for you. If you are looking for a publisher, you will need to prepare a book proposal.

You might say, "But I'm an author—an artist—my job is to write my book. I'm not a business person, why do I need to write a book proposal?" I think most writers feel that way. In a perfect world, we could be authors who just write and get discovered by publishers who sell thousands of our books and make us rich and famous. Unfortunately, we live in an imperfect world. We have to work at making ourselves known to those who are in the business of publishing the kinds of books we write. We need to convince publishers that they will benefit by publishing our book. But even that isn't enough. We will then have to convince book buyers that they will enjoy reading it. That means we need to do a book proposal.

A Book Proposal Is Like a Business Plan

Suppose you had invented a robotic maid and wanted it to be carried by a department store chain that would sell it to its customers. But the stores already carry a robotic maid in their housewares section—several brands, in fact. What's different and better about yours? Well, like the others, yours cleans the house but, unlike the others, it also does windows. Not only that, yours makes lunch and laughs at your jokes. But the people in that department store who make the decisions aren't going to know all that unless you tell them. You could give them a call but before they will make a commitment, they'll have to know more details. They are going to want to see some promotional material, the product itself, and possibly a demonstration. They'll have to be convinced that there are people out there who are just dying to have your particular robotic maid. It's your job to sell them on this wondrous machine.

It's not that much different when your product is a book. Writing a query letter isn't enough. It may get a publisher interested but he will still want to know how you intend to promote it. He will want to know what makes your book special and whether there is a market for it. He'll ask to see a book proposal and sample chapters or, sometimes, the entire manuscript.

For a nonfiction book, you can think of an idea, research the market, gather the facts, organize the material, write two or three chapters, and prepare a book proposal to send to a publisher before you even write the book. Then, if a publisher likes what he sees he may offer an advance. If you are like most writers, you have to earn a living. Having a cash advance might allow you to take a leave of absence from your job so that you can spend the time it takes to complete the book. The acquisitions editor of the publishing company will probably have some ideas of his own regarding what he wants to see in your book and will give you input to help you write a book that has a good chance of selling a lot of copies.

While the query letter for a novel and a nonfiction book are essentially the same in principle, the book proposal format presented here is designed primarily for the nonfiction book.

A book proposal for fiction does not contain as many parts. The proposal for a novel might have only the title page, a synopsis, and an author bio. If the author has written other books they should be listed along with information on how well they sold. Although there are exceptions, most agents and publishers want to see the entire manuscript of a novel rather than sample chapters.

A query letter should not be sent out until your book proposal has been completed. If you get a request from an agent or publisher to see your proposal, it should be ready so that you can send it right away. Interest may evaporate if you let a few weeks or months go by.

The advantages of writing a book proposal before you write the book are many. As you go through all the steps of the proposal you will learn:

- **How to focus on your subject**. If you have a descriptive title and can sum up your book in one short sentence, you probably have a clear idea of what your book is about.
- **How to describe your book to others**. By writing a synopsis, you will be able to get to the essence of the information contained in your book and explain it clearly.

- **How to organize your material**. Preparing a chapter-by-chapter outline of your book will help keep you on track as you write.
- **Whether you have a salable idea.** As you research the market potential, you will find out if your book is likely to find a wide audience.
- **How to sell yourself**. You will discover your qualifications for writing your book when you tell about your background and promotional skills. You can then build upon your strengths and do additional research in areas where you lack training or experience.
- **What your competition is** and if there are other books on the same subject. If you find books that are similar to yours, you may want to change yours in some way to make it stand out from the rest. You may even need to rethink whether you want to write this particular book at all.

Whether you have already written a book or are contemplating writing one, you will need to know what it takes to sell it. A book proposal can be prepared no matter what stage of writing you are in at the time. There are several factors that make for a bestselling nonfiction book. If you address all of these issues carefully and your book meets most of the following criteria, your chances of getting published will be greatly improved.

What Makes a Book Successful?

- The subject is timely and/or timeless; it is unique or presented in a unique way; it is interesting and appeals to a wide audience.
- The title is descriptive; it is intriguing or compelling, shocking or soothing, or in some way attracts attention.
- It is well written and carefully edited with attention paid to spelling, grammar, and sentence structure.
- If it is intended for the general reader, it avoids scientific or technical terminology unfamiliar to the layperson.
- It is easy to understand and enjoyable to read.
- The author is a professional in the field about which he is writing, is considered an authority on the subject, or has done extensive research on it.
- The material is well organized.
- The presentation is attractive, appealing, and professional looking.
- It has been diligently promoted and marketed.

Prepare your book proposal with all of the above factors in mind. The last item may not seem to be of concern to you as the author. But it is, because you will have to help promote and, in some cases, market your book no matter who the publisher is.

The format may differ somewhat depending on the publisher or agent to whom you will be presenting your proposal. For instance, some publishers require one sample chapter, some three or even more.

Some may ask that you put your name on every page and others may ask you not to. It's a good idea to modify your book proposal according to the standards of the person or company with whom you are dealing. You can find this information in a number of ways:

- By checking the publisher's listing in the latest issue of *Writer's Market* to see if they give this information
- By writing to the publishing company and asking for guidelines
- By checking out the publisher's website
- By emailing the acquisitions editor
- By calling the publishing company on the phone and asking

More and more, publishers are accepting queries and book proposals over the Internet. Their listing in one of the above reference books may tell you whether you can make submissions by email. That information might also be on their website.

The entire book proposal, except for the synopsis, should be double-spaced. On each page, place the section number and subject in the upper right corner. Below that put the title of your book and under that, the page number in that section.

The Book Proposal Contents Page

It is helpful to have a table of contents that shows at a glance what you have included in your proposal. At the top of the page, type "Book Proposal for [the title of your book]." Below that list the sections of the book proposal you have included, a list of illustrations, if any, and note which illustrations you are enclosing. After that, state which chapters you are sending. On the following page is an example.

BOOK PROPOSAL FOR

____

(title of book)

____

(subtitle)

by

____

(name of author)

I. Title Page
II. Synopsis
III. About the Author
IV. Market Potential
V. Competitive Works
VI. Chapter Outline
VII. List of Illustrations

Sample Illustrations (note what illustrations are included)

Chapters ____________________ (note the chapter numbers included)

____

Author's name

____

Address

____

City, State and Zip

____

Telephone and cell phone number

____

Email address

Title Page

Your title should be provocative and succinct. Publishers usually prefer short titles and they are easier for potential readers to remember. Notice how many books on bestseller lists have two- or three-word titles. Although there are some exceptions, such as *The Guernsey Literary and Potato Peel Pie Society,* only rarely do books on those lists have more than five words in the title. You can add a subtitle if you think that your short title doesn't tell enough about the book.

Do your best to get a hook into the title—something that will grab a reader's attention. Engage the emotions as much as possible such as in these titles: *Jewish Pirates of the Caribbean, Have a Little Faith,* and *Think and Grow Rich.*

The title should convey in some way what your book is about, especially if it is nonfiction. Some examples of titles that do this are: *Emotional Intelligence, Slaves in the Family, The Greatest Generation,* and *Ageless Body, Timeless Mind.*

Study the subject guide to *Books in Print* and note whether the subject you are writing on has been updated within the past few years. Also check *Forthcoming Books,* which details the books that publishers currently have in the works. Both are published by R.R. Bowker Co. Many book stores and public libraries have these lists on their computer.

Choose a title that has not been used before. Even though you can use an existing title because titles cannot be copyrighted, you wouldn't want your book confused with someone else's. If you want your book to stand out, it's best to select a title that is unique. If there are several books on the subject you have chosen, be sure that yours is different in important ways.

On the Title Page, put your title, subtitle (if any), and your name as the author. Below that write a brief description of your book. This is your primary sales pitch. Make it short and intriguing.

List the number of words you have written or expect to write. An average double-spaced manuscript page has around 300 to 350 words. The number of words on a book page varies widely depending on the size of the font and the page and the width of the margins. Most nonfiction books are between 170 and 300 pages. If your book will have fewer or more pages than these, be sure that there is a good reason for it. If there are fewer pages, don't pad. Every word should have a reason to be there. If there are more than 300 pages, be sure that you have not repeated yourself and that it requires that many pages to make your points.

Number the pages of the book proposal according to the section they are in, starting with page one in each new section.

On the following page is an example of a Title Page.

I. Title Page

A WOMAN'S WAY

A WOMAN'S WAY

The Stop-Smoking Book for Women

By Mary Embree

Smoking is a greater health hazard for women than for men
and it is harder for women to quit.

Number of words: 40,000

II. Synopsis

This is an overview or brief summary of the book. It should be about one and a half to two pages long and single-spaced. Place the book proposal section number and name on the top right corner of the page. Below that put the title of your book, and under that the page number.

Example:

II. SYNOPSIS
Title of Book
Page 1

Having a focused idea and being able to explain it in a few short paragraphs is essential. Tell the purpose of your book and what it will do for the reader.

The lead paragraph must grab the interest of the publishing company's acquisitions editor. Open with a powerful statement, startling statistics, or facts that will create interest or an emotional reaction.

Read book reviews, especially those on a similar subject as yours, and study book jackets as guides in developing the tone of the synopsis. As some agents and acquisition editors may not read beyond this point, it is important that you make the synopsis not only informative but interesting.

The synopsis should have a beginning, middle, and end, just as your book does. Tell how your book opens, what it is about, and how it ends. You may want to give some of the highlights, specific events, dialogue, or unknown facts.

At the bottom of the page, estimate the time needed to complete the book once the contract is signed.

Try to touch on most of the following in your synopsis:

- What kind of book is it? Tell whether it is a how-to book, a mystery, children's book, book of poetry, cookbook, historical novel, biography, and so forth.
- If it is a novel, what is the story? Who are the main characters?
- What is interesting and different about it? Is there an unusual twist? A unique point of view?
- How is it written? For example, if it is a novel, is it written in first person? If it's a nonfiction book, is it written for the layperson?

III. About the Author

This is also called Author's Background and Promotional Skills or Biographical Information. It is a narrative statement of your qualifications, experience, and reasons for writing the book. Do not send a resume or curriculum vitae. Your bio should be no more than two pages long.

Tell about yourself, list other books you have written, and explain your promotional skills such as public speaking, television or radio appearances, or seminars you have conducted on the subject. Suggest the names of prominent figures or authorities who may endorse your book. If you already have contacted them and they have agreed, be sure to mention it.

To see if you have covered everything, use the following checklist.

- ☐ Education; special training
- ☐ Experience in the field you are writing about
- ☐ Other books, articles, scripts, or papers you have written
- ☐ Public speaking experience. Seminar presenter? Teacher? Politician? Actor?
- ☐ Personal information, especially when applicable to what you are writing
- ☐ Marketing or promotional experience
- ☐ Reason for writing this book
- ☐ Endorsements

All of the above may not apply to you and your book. If you are writing a novel, a university degree may be unimportant. If you are writing a nonfiction book regarding a specific field of interest it will be important to show that you have training and/or experience in that field. Some authors also send a picture of themselves but that is not necessary.

IV. Market Potential

Research the demographics and statistics of potential readers. For example: "The number of women living with children whose father was absent was over 10 million in 2002." This number will be significant if your book is about how a mother who is rearing her children alone can help them feel secure, excel in school, and make positive choices. These single mothers are all potential readers.

If your book were about motorcycles, you would want to have statistics on how many people own motorcycles. You would also want to tell how many motorcycle clubs, dealers, and accessory stores there are. Their club members and customers are potential readers and your book could be sold through their club, store, or dealership.

For my own first book, *A Woman's Way: The Stop Smoking Book for Women,* I did a lot of my research in hospital libraries and, among other important facts, found out how many American women are smoking, what percentage of them want to quit, the health statistics for female vs. male smokers and the health effects on the fetuses, infants, and children of women smokers. As I was working on the book in the early 1990s, there wasn't as much information on the Internet as there is now. And very little research had been done at that time on women's smoking, especially in the United States.

In addition to bookstores, other outlets for this book were women's clinics, gynecologist's offices, public health centers, and hospitals. Each facility ordered multiple copies of *A Woman's Way* for doctors, nurses, and therapists to give to their patients who smoked.

Knowing the possible outlets for your book at the time you are preparing your book proposal gives you a distinct advantage. Don't assume that the publisher will know how and where to market your book. You may have ideas the publisher hasn't even thought of.

V. Competitive Works

Research other books on the same subject. They are your competition. Borrow or buy books that may be similar to yours and read them. Choose four or five and list each by title, author, publisher, the year published, the number of pages, and the price. Write a brief synopsis of each one and explain how yours is different. Be sure the books you list are recent. Very old books will not be considered comparable.

VI. Chapter Outline

Prepare a Table of Contents with chapter titles but without page numbers. Under each chapter title write a paragraph or two explaining what it is about. This indicates that you have a clear grasp of your subject and have planned exactly how and in what order you will present your information. Here's an example from my book proposal:

Chapter 1: A Cigarette Is NOT a Friend

Women often think of a cigarette as a friend, something that is always there when they are nervous, emotionally upset, lonely, or even celebrating. Smoking is a different addiction in women than it is in men. It is more damaging to their health and it's harder for them to quit.

Chapter 2: Pregnancy, PMS, and Menopause

This chapter explains the danger to the fetus of a pregnant woman who smokes. It also tells how smoking can intensify premenstrual tension, and the increased tension, like a vicious cycle, makes it harder for women to quit. There is evidence that smoking can also bring on an early menopause.

VII. List of Illustrations

If you have photographs, drawings, graphs, charts, maps, or other illustrations that will become a part of this work, list and describe each one. Also include samples.

Sample Chapters

You will be sending between one and three completed chapters, depending on what the publisher asks for. Always send the first chapter because publishers usually want to know how you get into your subject. The first ten pages of your book are crucial. Actually, the first page is crucial, even the first few lines. You must grab the reader's interest right away. Here are some lines from the first pages of bestselling and/or classic novels:

My father has asked me to be the fourth corner at the Joy Luck Club. I am to replace my mother, whose seat at the mahjong table has been empty since she died two months ago. My father thinks she was killed by her own thoughts.

➤ *The Joy Luck Club,* by Amy Tan

The large ballroom was crowded with familiar ghosts come to help celebrate her birthday. Kate Blackwell watched them mingle with the flesh-and-blood people, and in her mind, the scene was a dreamlike fantasy as the visitors from another time and place glided around the dance floor with the unsuspecting guests in black tie and long, shimmering evening gowns.

➤ *Master of the Game,* by Sidney Sheldon

It is a truth universally acknowledged that a single man in possession of a good fortune must be in want of a wife.

➤ *Pride and Prejudice,* by Jane Austen

And these are from nonfiction books:

When the door opened in front of him, my visitor knew he was being led into a secret CIA apartment. But which of us was really being led? As he took my welcoming hand I had no idea that it was to drag me and my service into a labyrinth so complex that even today, more than forty years later, my successors have still not found their way through its twists and turns.

➤ *Spy Wars: Moles, Mysteries, and Deadly Games,* by Tennent H. Bagley

My father and mother should have stayed in New York where they met and married and where I was born. . . . When I look back on my childhood I wonder how I survived at all.

➤ *Angela's Ashes,* by Frank McCourt

As a boy, I never knew where my mother was from—where she was born, who her parents were. When I asked she'd say, "God made me." When I asked if she was white, she'd say, "I'm light-skinned," and change the subject. She raised twelve black children and sent us all to college . . . "

➤ *The Color of Water: A Black Man's Tribute to His White Mother,* by James McBride

The most famous first line of all time is "It was the best of times, it was the worst of times" from the classic *A Tale of Two Cities* by Charles Dickens. That line draws you in and sets the tone for the entire book.

The other two chapters you submit should be the ones you believe are the most important or most interesting. If you have a dynamite closing chapter, include it. Don't worry about giving away the ending. Your goal is to sell your book.

Book Proposal Checklist

Before you send your book proposal off to the publisher, double-check that you have done the following.

- ☐ Included a cover letter addressed to the person who requested the proposal, stating what you are sending and why
- ☐ Checked the spelling of the editor's name, company name, and address
- ☐ Proofread all of the material you are planning to send
- ☐ Included any additional material such as illustrations and everything else that was requested
- ☐ Made the margins at least one inch wide on the cover letter and all pages of the proposal
- ☐ Included your name, address, telephone and fax numbers, and email address in the letter
- ☐ Signed your cover letter
- ☐ Included the title of your book on each page of the proposal
- ☐ Affixed the appropriate postage on the package
- ☐ Enclosed a stamped self-addressed envelope for a response and/or return of the proposal

CHAPTER THIRTEEN

The Query Letter

Three questions are essential to all just criticism: What is the author's object? How far has he accomplished it? How far is that object worthy of approbation?

➤ Nathaniel Parker Willis [1835]

The query letter is usually one page long and single-spaced. If you absolutely cannot include all of the information on one page, go to a second page. The margins must be at least one inch wide on the sides and three-quarters inch wide at the bottom.

A query letter should contain a condensed version of the major points you made in your book proposal. If your book is nonfiction, it is always a good idea to write your book proposal and a few chapters before sending out query letters. Publishers of novels usually want to see the entire manuscript, not just a book proposal. There are exceptions, but they are rare. Preparing a proposal first will help you compose your query and, if an agent or publisher is interested in your idea and asks for more, you will be ready.

The information you will need to include in the query letter is virtually the same whether you are seeking an agent or a publisher. If you are sending the query directly to a publisher, simply change it accordingly. Instead of asking for representation, ask if they would be interested in publishing your book. Again, tailor your letter to the particular publisher you are contacting, being sure that they publish the kind of book you are writing.

How to Choose a Publisher

In the chapter on agents I made suggestions on how to find the right agent for your book. However, you may choose to query a publisher directly and need to know which ones publish your kind of book. *Writer's Market* has that information but there are so many publishers listed that it will be very time-consuming to examine them all. You could also go to the library and look in *Literary Marketplace* to check the Type of Publication and the Subject Indexes.

A shortcut to choosing the right publisher for your book is to go to a bookstore and look in the section that has the kinds of books you are writing. Notice the titles that catch your eye. Pick up those books and briefly study them. Read the chapter titles on the contents page of nonfiction books. Read the first page of novels. When you find a book that has something in common with yours, write down the title, author, publishing company, and the year the book was published. You could also do this kind of research on Amazon.com. Often they have sample pages that you can read online. Study bestseller lists, too, because the publishers of those books are probably doing a good job of promoting their books. If you find a book on that list that is in the same genre as yours, you will want to contact the publisher of it.

Then check those publishers' listings in the above-mentioned directories. There you will find out whether they want a query letter first or if they will accept a book proposal on first contact. You will learn where to send your letter and who to address it to. Many publishers now have a website that you can go to in order to find out more about them. Often they will have their books listed with brief synopses of them. Spend whatever time it takes to learn about the publishing company including what kinds of books they publish, what they are looking for, if they want to see an outline, sample chapters, photos, or anything else and, most important of all, whether they accept submissions from authors. Major publishing houses such as Random House, Simon & Schuster, Harcourt, and Harper Collins, only accept agented submissions. It is a waste of your time and money to send queries or book proposals to publishers who refuse to look at manuscripts that have not been submitted by agents. Even though these publishers are listed in *Writer's Market*, you would not choose them unless you have some other way of getting their attention, such as knowing someone on the inside who will clear a path for you.

Many publishers now accept submissions by email. If they list an email address, you may contact them through the Internet asking who you should send your query letter to and whether they would also like to see sample chapters, synopses, and so forth. It's always a good idea to find out who the current acquisitions editor is. The person whose name is listed in the directories may have left the company since the book was published. When you address your letter, check and double-check the spelling of the editor's name to be sure that it is accurate. I have heard of editors who threw the query letter into the trash if their name was misspelled. You'll have a better chance of getting his attention if you start off on the right foot.

Sometimes you can send both your query and any additional material that publishers want to see as an email with attachments. It saves on paper, postage, and time to do it that way. Proofread everything you send whether by email or through the postal service. Even a brief note sent by email should have proper spelling, punctuation, sentence structure, and grammar. People often get sloppy when they send emails. That may be fine when you are writing your friends or family, but when you are contacting an agent or publisher, you should be professional. You will be judged by what and how you write.

When you write your query letter, imagine what the literary agent or publisher's acquisitions editor who will be reading it will want to know, and answer the following questions.

What do you want? Explain your purpose for writing: you have a manuscript on (subject matter) and you are seeking agency representation or a book publisher. The first paragraph should also include your "hook."

Why have you chosen this agency or publishing company? Show that you have done your research by stating your reasons for choosing that particular agent: author recommendation, the agent's reputation, the agent represents similar works, and so forth. If you are sending this to a publisher, mention that they have published similar types of books. If there is one that your book compares to in some way (for example, a historical novel, biography, how-to, or children's book) name the title and explain the similarities and differences.

What is your book about? State the title and describe your book in a brief synopsis. This should not take up more than two or three lines. Read book jackets and ads for ideas.

What is your background? Explain your qualifications for writing this book. Are you an expert in this particular field? List other published works. If this is your first book, what else have you written? Television or film scripts? Magazine articles? Scientific papers?

What was your reason for writing this book? Explain whether it is new information on the subject, a unique approach, or an unusual story. Tell why you wanted to write it.

Who will want to read it? Target your audience so that a publisher will know how to market your book. Research is imperative here.

What do you have to show me? Explain what you would like to send. If you have written a nonfiction book, ask if you may send a book proposal. If it is a novel, offer to send a synopsis of it or the full manuscript.

Your query letter should be concise so choose your words carefully and check for spelling, grammatical construction, and so on. This is the first example of your writing the agent or publisher will see, so make it the best it can be. Maintain a positive attitude about your creative work. Don't be apologetic or defensive. And if you want a reply one way or the other, always send a self-addressed stamped envelope.

Try to keep your query letter short. I have heard of three- and four-page query letters that got the attention of a publisher but they are the exceptions to the rule.

Here are some examples to follow as you write your query letter.

The First Paragraph

It's always a good idea to begin your letter with your "hook." Make your opening paragraph as powerful as you can. Include the title of your book in this paragraph. This is the most important part of your letter so make sure it's a grabber.

Here are two examples:

> One of the most baffling murder cases of the century began on a hot August night in Malibu with the brutal slaying of a beautiful porno star in the bedroom of noted TV evangelist Randy Saint. In *Saint and Sinner* I dissect the sloppy investigative work of the prosecution that put the wrong man on death row.

> Since ancient times, healers have told us our minds and bodies are one. Now, some amazing new research has proven this connection. A number of highly respected scientists and physicians have documented "miracle" cures using the power of the mind. This instant healing is something everyone can do and in my book, *If You Can Love, You Can Heal,* I explain how.

The Body of the Letter

Briefly synopsize your book. Include in the description of your book some of the more interesting passages, unknown facts, or your own involvement in the story, if pertinent. Here are two examples:

> Smoking is not the same addiction in women as it is in men. By the year 2000, women's death rate from smoking surpassed men's. This book addresses those differences and shows women how they can quit for good—without gaining weight.

> Born into wealth on a cotton plantation in the Old South sixteen years before the start of the Civil War, Susanna Campbell was given everything she could ever want except her parent's love. The delicate and beautiful girl was closer

> to her black nanny than she was to her own family. Still, no one could have predicted that Susanna would spend the Civil War years risking her life hiding runaway slaves. This true story is told through her recently discovered journals.

Explain your reasons for writing the book and tell a little about yourself.

> As a physical therapist with a masters degree in psychology, I have found that the most valuable help for a child recovering from a serious accident is a therapeutic process I developed after my own devastating accident. Using this procedure, children get well in half the usual time.

Tell what the market for the book is and, in the last paragraph, describe what you would like to send. For help in writing the query letter go to your book proposal and highlight the most important points.

The Closing Paragraph

Describe what you would like to send. Your research may have indicated whether the agent or publisher would like to see the whole manuscript, a book proposal, or a synopsis. If it is a book proposal, explain briefly what it consists of, for example:

> I would like to send you my book proposal along with three sample chapters, a total of sixty-five pages.

Query Letter Checklist

Before you send off your letter, look over this checklist to be sure you have done the following:

- ☐ Gotten the name of the current acquisitions editor
- ☐ Checked the spelling of the editor's name, company name, and address
- ☐ Proofread the query letter and all other material you are planning to send
- ☐ Made the margins at least one inch wide
- ☐ Included your name, address, telephone and fax numbers, and email address in the letter
- ☐ Made a compelling statement and mentioned the title of your book in the first paragraph
- ☐ Given your experience, credentials, and/or reason for writing the book
- ☐ Described your book
- ☐ Stated who the intended audience is and, if known, how to reach those readers

- ☐ Stated what action you are asking for in the last paragraph
- ☐ Signed your letter
- ☐ Affixed the appropriate postage on the envelope or package
- ☐ Enclosed a stamped self-addressed envelope for a response

CHAPTER FOURTEEN

The Literary Agency Agreement

A verbal agreement isn't worth the paper it's written on.

➤ Attributed to Samuel Goldwyn

Any written agreement can be a legally enforceable contract. The following information should not be construed as legal advice, merely a discussion of what to expect in agreements you make with an agent, publisher, or collaborator, and what to watch out for. Because laws and procedures are different in different states, countries, and industries, and are subject to change, you are advised to get qualified legal advice before signing any agreement. Sometimes authors are so excited about finding an agent or a publisher who is interested in their book that they will sign just about anything. Remember the old saying, "Act in haste, repent at leisure," and proceed with caution.

Once you have found an agent who you think is the right one to represent you and your works, and that agent has offered representation, there are a number of questions you should ask.

The Association of Authors' Representatives, Inc. (AAR) has a list of twenty-two topics they suggest you discuss. Until you know more about the literary agency, it is not advisable to sign any contract.

Questions to Ask before You Sign

Find out if the agent is a member of the Association of Author's Representatives. All members must abide by a Canon of Ethics and satisfy the requirements for AAR membership, which include experience in the field. To qualify for membership the agent must have been "principally responsible for executed agreements concerning the grant of publication, translation or performance rights in ten different literary properties during the eighteen-month period preceding application." Here are some other questions to ask.

- How long has your agency been in business and how many people are employed in the agency?
- Who in the agency will actually be handling my work?
- Will that person keep me apprised of the work the agency is doing on my behalf?
- Will you provide editorial input and career guidance?
- Do you provide submission lists and copies of publishers' rejection letters?
- Will you consult with me on all offers?
- What is your commission? (Most charge 15 percent for basic sales to U.S. publishers.)
- How do you process and disburse client funds?
- Do you charge for expenses incurred in handling my work such as postage, phone charges, and copying costs and, if so, will you itemize such expenses for me?
- Do you issue annual 1099 tax forms?
- What do you expect of me as your client?

Taking the time to discuss those matters will help smooth the relationship with your agent. Before getting involved you must know what the agent's responsibility is and what yours is. One complaint agents make is that their clients expect them to be available to speak with them at all times. They also grumble that authors think agents aren't doing their job if they don't get them a deal with a publisher. But, the agents say, some manuscripts just aren't marketable for any number of reasons and they have so many clients that they can't talk to each one every day on the phone. They need time to contact publishers. That's in the best interest of the client.

Many writers say that after they signed the agreement with their agent they never heard from him again. The agent wouldn't even return their phone calls. Writers are often disappointed that their agent did not take an interest in their writing career.

Even if you feel that everything you wanted to know was addressed, other questions will come up during the course of your agent/author relationship, and maintaining clear and friendly lines of communication will make it easier on both of you.

For a small fee the AAR will furnish you a list of their members. Agents are listed according to their specialization: L = Literary, D = Dramatic, and C = Children. They will not make recommendations to authors seeking representation, though.

Not all agents supply an agreement or contract for you to sign. Often the agent and author agree to terms informally. It's always a good idea to have the terms spelled out in a memo or letter from your agent. If the agent does not prepare an agreement, you can write one, based upon your understanding of the relationship, and send it to the agent asking if you are correct in your assumptions. That way there are likely to be fewer misunderstandings.

If you are offered a contract, discuss anything that is unclear to you with the agent and be sure that you understand it before you sign. Get as much information as you can before you sign any agreement with an agent (or anyone, for that matter). There is a great deal of valuable contract information in *The Writer's Legal Guide: An Authors Guild Desk Reference,* by Tad Crawford and Kay Murray, and in *Business and Legal Forms for Authors and Self-Publishers* by Tad Crawford. Other good resources are *How to Get Happily Published* by Judith Appelbaum and *How to Be Your Own Literary Agent* by Richard Curtis.

Important facets of an agency agreement are the following.

The Grant of Authority

Set limits on your agent's authority to act in your behalf. You should have ultimate control over the sale of your rights. Agents should not sign a contract and bind you to it.

The Agent's Obligation

What will your agent do for you? This should be spelled out clearly. The agent should use her "best efforts" to sell your work and to act in "good faith" on your behalf. She should make a conscientious effort to sell your work. She should submit all offers to you, whether or not she thinks you should accept any of them. The agent should keep in touch with you and return your phone calls. You can't expect a busy, active agent to spend hours on the phone with you. But if you have not heard from her for a few months, it's reasonable to think she's forgotten you, and a call to her would be in order.

The deals you make and the contracts you sign are your own personal business and your agent should keep your financial affairs private and confidential. It is unethical for your agent to brag about the deal she got for you or the advance you received. Such loose talk could jeopardize future dealings with publishers.

Your agent should counsel and advise you, giving you the benefit of her experience. If she doesn't take the time to explain to you why you should or should not accept a particular offer, she isn't doing her job.

As the relationship between the agent and author can become an intensely personal one, you may want to be sure that the agency will not arbitrarily assign you to another agent in the future. Employees come and go and if the agent with whom you have established rapport leaves the agency, you may wish to terminate the agency relationship. Will the agency ask your permission before transferring you to someone else? This is a matter that should be clarified at the time you sign the agreement.

The Author's Obligation

Your obligation is to pay a commission when your agent sells your work. You may decide you want an "exclusive agency" relationship wherein you would not owe the agent a commission if you sold the work yourself. This might be the best kind of arrangement for you if you have extensive contacts within the publishing industry and have reason to believe that you could very well make a deal with a publisher on the golf course. (And probably more deals are made there than are made in offices.) Under this type of agreement, however, you must compensate your agent if another agent gets the deal for you. In that case, you would owe commissions to both agents.

Most agents want an "exclusive sale" agreement where you would be obligated to pay a commission no matter who sold your work. For most new authors that is probably okay. But beware of any arrangement where you end up selling your future.

Make sure your agent is representing you for a particular property or for specific works. In no case should you agree to letting him represent everything you have ever written or will write in the future.

Warranties

Both you and your agent need to warrant that you are free to enter the agreement, that you will be able to fully perform your obligation, and that you do not have any other contracts that will conflict with the provisions of the agency agreement.

Just as writers can tell horror stories about their agents, agents have some hair-raising tales about their clients. They've had clients who plagiarized someone else's work and represented it as their own, or who sold their work themselves without notifying them.

Commissions

Literary agents whose main client base consists of authors of books usually charge 15 percent. Agents who represent film or television writers generally charge a

10 percent commission. The Writers Guild of America (WGA) maintains a list of signatory agents who represent material such as screenplays, teleplays, stories, treatments, plot outlines, formats, breakdowns, sketches, and narrations. Here is an excerpt from the WGA Agreement with Agents:

> The Guild disapproves of the practice followed by certain agencies of charging a "reading fee" or some similar fee to writers who submit literary material to them. Accordingly, the Guild will not be willing to list any such agency. The only monies listed agencies may collect from their clients is a 10 percent commission after successfully negotiating a deal.

As the author of a manuscript for a book, you would not ordinarily go to a WGA agent. Some exceptions might be if you have written a novel that would translate well onto the screen or a nonfiction book that could be made into a film or TV documentary. But even then, most experienced writers and agents will tell you that your best chance of getting it produced is to get it published as a book first.

As this is about getting your book completed and published, you will be seeking a literary agent who represents authors, not scriptwriters. There is no guild that tells those agents what they must charge. The fee is negotiable, however, and if you have extensive contacts and can help your agent get a publishing deal, you may be able to negotiate a 10 percent commission. For foreign sales the commission ranges up to 20 percent. That is because the agent often has to split the commission with an agent in another country.

Your agent may also ask for an advance of about $100 for some out-of-pocket expenses such as postage, long-distance calling, and photocopying. That is not an unreasonable request and most agents will give you an accounting of how the money was spent.

The agency agreement usually provides for the publisher to pay your royalties directly to the agent, who takes his percentage out and writes a check to you for the balance. As your agent will likely be able to read and understand a royalty statement better than you, that puts him in the position of monitoring the publisher.

Three things that should definitely be in the written agreement are (1) that your agent pays you your share promptly, (2) that you are allowed to examine the account books at any time, and (3) that your money is kept in a client trust account, separate from the agency's own funds.

Multiple Agents

As your agent may not be able to represent you for film and television sales, you may wish to sign with a WGA-approved agent in addition to your literary agent. You are not required to grant any one agent the authority over your entire bundle of rights. You can have different types of agents representing your different types of rights. You will need to specify the type of work the agent will be representing and be sure that you are not giving the agent any later works you may produce or for which you already have an established market. You may want the agent to represent your book but not your magazine articles or scripts.

The Contract Term

You may want to give your agent a definite amount of time to represent you. Usually one year is sufficient to find out whether the agent can sell your work, whether you are compatible, and whether you trust him enough to want to continue to work with him.

An agent may want more time because it may take many years before an author begins to earn significant income from her writing. If you still feel comfortable with your agent after a year, even if he hasn't made a deal, you may want to stay with him.

Terminating the Agreement

You may not want to commit to a year or to any definite period of time. You may want the freedom to terminate the relationship at any time after giving a thirty-day notice. Then if it doesn't seem to be working out, you can move on to another agent.

Some agency agreements contain post-termination clauses stating that they are owed a commission if you or another agent sells your work to a publisher within ninety days after termination of the agreement. If your agent has been working hard trying to sell your manuscript and has made a number of impressive contacts, that's a reasonable and fair request.

Learning More

Whenever possible, speak to an author the agent has represented and ask whether there were any problems with that agent before you sign an agreement for representation. The American Society of Journalists and Authors, the National Writers Association, and the National Writers Union maintain files on agents their members have worked with.

The NWU has a Preferred Literary Agent Agreement and a guide, "Understanding the Author-Agent Relationship," that are available to members. Their guide is an educational tool to help you understand and evaluate your agreement. It explains that an author's work is a bundle of individual rights including hardcover print rights, paperback print rights, electronic database rights, interactive software rights, foreign translation rights, television adaptation rights, and audio cassette rights, to name a few. Collectively, they form the copyright to the author's work. The author owns these rights until she signs them away. Each right may be licensed or transferred independently of the others. The NWU explains, "this principle is known as the 'Doctrine of Divisibility' and is a cornerstone of U.S. copyright law."

Agent agreements should be "work-specific," advises the NWU. Be wary of any agreement that gives the agent automatic authority to represent future works that you may produce for a publisher. The agent's authority should be clearly identified in the original contract.

Agents sometimes offer "work-for-hire" agreements in which the author gives up the copyright of her own creation. Work-for-hire and all-rights agreements may indicate that the agent is not really an agent but a packager.

Also beware if an agent represents both parties in a collaboration agreement. That raises the potential for a conflict of interest.

Whatever agreement you make with your agent, be sure that you both understand it completely and that the details are in writing.

The following is a sample of an Author-Agent Contract, reproduced by permission from *Business and Legal Forms for Authors and Self-Publishers* by Tad Crawford (Allworth Press, 2015).

Author—Agent Contract

AGREEMENT, entered into as of this ____ day of ______, 20___, between ________________ (hereinafter referred to as the "Author"), located at ______________________________, and ____ (hereinafter referred to as the "Agent"), located at ____.

WHEREAS, the Author is an established author of proven talents; and

WHEREAS, the Author wishes to have an agent represent him or her in marketing certain rights enumerated herein; and

WHEREAS, the Agent is capable of marketing the writing created by the Author; and

WHEREAS, the Agent wishes to represent the Author;

NOW, THEREFORE, in consideration of the foregoing premises and the mutual covenants hereinafter set forth and other valuable consideration, the parties hereto agree as follows:

1. **Agency**. The Author appoints the Agent to act as his or her representative:
   (A) in the following geographical area ____
   (B) for the following markets: [ ] Book publishing [ ] Magazines [ ] Television [ ] Motion Picture [ ] Other, specified as ____
   (C) to be the Author's [ ] exclusive [ ] nonexclusive agent in the area and markets indicated.
   (D) Electronic rights are [ ] outside the scope of this agency contract [ ] covered by this agency contract insofar as the sale of such rights is incidental to the sale of nonelectronic rights [ ] covered by this agency contract. For purposes of this agreement, electronic rights are defined as rights in the digitized form of works that can be encoded, stored, and retrieved from such media as computer disks, CD-ROM, computer databases, and network servers.

   Any rights not granted to the Agent are reserved to the Author.

2. **Best Efforts.** The Agent agrees to use his or her best efforts in submitting the Author's work for the purpose of securing assignments for the Author. The Agent shall negotiate the terms of any assignment that is offered, but the Author may reject any assignment if he or she finds the terms thereof unacceptable.

3. **Samples.** The Author shall provide the Agent with such samples of work as are from time to time necessary for the purpose of securing assignments. These samples shall remain the property of the Author and be returned on termination of this Agreement.

4. **Term.** This Agreement shall take effect as of the date first set forth above, and remain in full force and effect for a term of one year, unless terminated as provided in Paragraph 10.

5. **Commissions.** The Agent shall be entitled to a ________ percent commission for work obtained by the Agent during the term of this Agreement and a ________ percent commission for work obtained by the Author during the term of this Agreement, except that no commission shall be payable for the following types of work obtained by the Author ____.

   It is understood by both parties that no commissions shall be paid on assignments rejected by the Author or for which the Author fails to receive payment, regardless of the reason payment is not made. Further, no commissions shall be payable for any part of the billing that is due to expenses incurred by the Author and reimbursed by the client. In the event that a flat fee is paid by the client, [ ] the Agent's commission shall be payable only on the fee as reduced for expenses [ ] the Agent's commission shall be payable on the full fee.

6. **Billing.** The Agent shall be responsible for all billings.

7. **Payments.** The Agent shall make all payments due within ________ days of receipt of any fees covered by this Agreement. Such payments due shall be deemed trust funds and shall not be intermingled with funds belonging to the Agent. Late payments shall be accompanied by interest calculated at the rate of _____ percent per month thereafter.

8. **Accountings.** The Agent shall send copies of statements of account received by the Agent to the Author when rendered. If requested, the Agent shall also provide the Author with semiannual accountings showing all income for the period, the clients' names and addresses, the fees paid, the dates of payment, the amounts on which the Agent's commissions are to be calculated, and the sums due less those amounts already paid.

9. **Inspection of the Books and Records.** The Agent shall keep the books and records with respect to payments due each party at his or her place of business and permit the other party to inspect these books and records during normal business hours on the giving of reasonable notice.

10. **Termination.** This Agreement may be terminated by either party by giving thirty (30) days written notice to the other party. In the event of the bankruptcy or insolvency of the Agent, this Agreement shall also terminate. The rights and obligations under Paragraphs 3, 6, 7, 8, and 9 shall survive termination, provided that in the event of termination the Author shall have the right to have payments (less commissions) paid directly to the Author rather than to the Agent as set forth in Paragraph 7.

11. **Assignment.** This Agreement shall not be assigned by either of the parties hereto. It shall be binding on and inure to the benefit of the successors, admininstrators, executors, or heirs of the Agent and Author.

12. **Arbitration.** Any disputes arising under this Agreement shall be settled by arbitration before __________ under the rules of the American Arbitration Association in the City of __________________, except that the parties shall have the right to go to court for claims of $_______ or less. Any award rendered by the arbitrator may be entered in any court having jurisdiction thereof.

13. **Notices.** All notices shall be given to the parties at their respective addresses set forth above.
____

14. **Independent Contractor Status.** Both parties agree that the Agent is acting as an independent contractor. This Agreement is not an employment agreement, nor does it constitute a joint venture or partnership between the Author and Agent.

15. **Amendments and Merger.** All amendments to this Agreement must be written. This Agreement incorporates the entire understanding of the parties.

16. **Governing Law.** This Agreement shall be governed by the laws of the State of______________.

IN WITNESS WHEREOF, the parties have signed this Agreement as of the date set forth above.

Author ____________________________________ Agent ____________

CHAPTER FIFTEEN

The Book Publishing Contract

Publishing is an act of commerce. To stay in business, you must profit.

➢ Richard Snyder, chairman, Simon & Schuster

Many changes have taken place in the publishing world over the past few years that have made the publishing contract more complex than ever. As I am not a lawyer, I cannot give you legal advice, but I can alert you to some of the elements to consider.

Technology is the major reason for the ever-changing publishing contract. The twentieth century brought with it many new and different ways to record and transmit written works. Along with audiotape and videotape machines came radio, film, and television. Following on the heels of photocopying machines were personal computers, scanners, and printers. The computer made the Internet possible and that development made copyrighted material available to everyone on a massive scale. This explosion of new technologies has presented the enormous challenge of defining and protecting authors' rights to their literary creations. And the twenty-first century promises even more unimaginable advances over the already complex machinery and future business of communication.

Among the rights that must be spelled out in a publishing contract are paperback rights, book club rights, photocopying and facsimile rights, microfilm rights, audio rights, motion picture and television rights, and the various categories of electronic rights which are evolving so fast that they defy legal definitions. As media, technologies, and markets change, a contract that works today is out of date tomorrow.

The following is an overview to familiarize you with the kinds of agreements that have been used.

Before you sign any agreement with a publisher, be sure you know what you are signing. If you have an active, qualified agent with current contacts in the publishing field, he can help you understand the details of your contract. If you do not have an agent, it would be wise to get some legal advice from an attorney who specializes in, or at least is familiar with, publishing law. If neither of those options is available to you, get a recently published book that contains information on publishers' contracts.

The clearest and most comprehensive book I have found on writers' rights and the law is *The Writer's Legal Guide: An Authors Guild Desk Reference.* It is written by Tad Crawford, who is an attorney, book publisher, and author, and Kay Murray, formerly the general counsel and assistant director of the Authors Guild, which is the nation's largest organization of published authors. *Publishers Weekly* calls the *Guide* an indispensable handbook for anyone who writes. In addition to information on negotiating a book deal and protecting your rights, it covers many other facets of the business of writing.

Another informative reference is *Business and Legal Forms for Authors and Self-Publishers* by Tad Crawford, which contains, among other agreements, a standard book publishing contract. Both books explain the fine points of the contract including the grant of rights, compensation, artistic control, and more. A negotiation checklist is included to help you understand and negotiate your agreement.

If you can qualify for membership, you will benefit by joining the Authors Guild. It is the nation's leading advocate for writers' interests, providing legal assistance and web services to its members. You may qualify on the basis of being a book author or freelance writer. Dues are $90 per year. When you join you will receive the Guild's *Model Trade Book Contract and Guide* and the added benefit of having attorneys review and advise you about your contract at no charge.

"Electronic Rights" is a term that can have many meanings with the proliferation of new technologies. It is particularly challenging because things are changing too fast for settled legal definitions. There are no "standard" electronic rights clauses in publishing contracts. Be sure this is addressed in very specific language in your contract. It should be spelled out clearly who owns the right to exploit a book through a "publishing-on-demand" system, for example. Also called"print-on-demand" (POD), these computer-based systems are changing the way books are distributed and sold. In some areas the system is in place whereby a bookstore customer can order an "ebook" from a catalog. The book can then be printed out from an electronic database, bound, and delivered on the spot.

"Advance against Royalties" is money the author gets before the book is published. The author's goal should be getting paid at the rate of half upon signing the agreement and half upon delivery of an acceptable manuscript of the book. That money is not a no-strings gift from the publisher. It is deducted from future royalties on the sale of the book. Thus an author may not receive any royalty checks for a year or more.

How important is an advance? It depends on a number of factors. If an advance will allow you the freedom to work on your book instead of working a full-time job, it could be very important. Also, if you receive a significant advance, the publisher will want to protect its investment by advertising and promoting your book.

"Royalties on Publisher's Editions" is the share of sales the author receives. In the past this was often a percentage of the retail or cover price of the book. For example, if the price printed on the book cover was $10 and the author's royalty rate was 10 percent, the author received a dollar for each copy sold. A more frequent arrangement now is for the percentage to be based on the "invoice price," which is what the publisher receives from bookstores and wholesalers. Because a publisher may give them a discount of 40 percent or more, the publisher's net on a $10 book might be $6, in which case the author would receive 60 cents per book. Generally, an author should resist royalties based on net proceeds as they can be considerably less than royalties based on the retail price. If retail price isn't used, the author should seek a higher royalty rate on net proceeds to make the two methods of calculation yield similar royalty amounts.

"Delivery of Manuscript" has to do with the date and form in which the author has agreed to deliver the completed manuscript. The publisher may ask for a computer disk containing the manuscript in a word-processing program and a hard copy (a printout).

"Artwork, Permissions, Index, and Other Materials" may include original art, illustrations, photos, charts, an index, bibliography, contents page, introduction, etc. It may also involve authorizations, permissions, and endorsements.

"Publisher's Rights on Delivery" allows the publisher to terminate the agreement without further obligation to the author if the publisher finds the manuscript or any of the materials unacceptable. The publisher may give the author the opportunity to make revisions or corrections and resubmit. This clause also gives the publisher the right to terminate the agreement if the material is not delivered on time. In this case, the author will probably be required to repay the publisher for any advance she has received. The publisher may terminate the contract if changed conditions have adversely affected the salability of the work but, in that event, the author is usually allowed to keep the advance.

Publication

This section deals with authorizing the publisher to edit and revise the work, to design the book, set the price, print, advertise, and promote it, among other things. It may also state the date of publication, the number of free copies the author will receive and provide for revisions.

Copyright

This states that the publisher shall apply for a copyright in the name of the author and place the notice in the book. It also has to do with possible copyright infringement and how the parties may handle litigation.

Accounting

The publisher sets up a formal system of accounting where it credits the author's account with royalties and any other payments and debits it for the advance, returned books, etc. This also states the author's audit rights.

Agency

The author authorizes and appoints the agent to act on behalf of the author to collect and receive payments and other communications from the publisher.

Warranties, Representations, and Indemnities

The author is asked to guarantee that his work will not result in a lawsuit and agrees to bear all costs of defending a claim if one is made. The author warrants that the work is not in public domain because, if anyone can freely publish it, the publisher doesn't have to acquire the rights from the author in the first place. The author also states that he is the sole proprietor of the work and has the authority to enter the agreement and grant the rights.

It is your job, as an author, to protect your rights. You can't expect anyone else to do that for you. That is why you must educate yourself about copyrights, literary agents, book publishers, and each and every contract and agreement you may be asked to sign. Each agreement must be fine-tuned to suit the author, the publisher, and the project.

The following is a sample of a book publishing contract, reproduced by permission from *Business and Legal Forms for Authors and Self-Publishers* by Tad Crawford (Allworth Press).

Book Publishing Contract

AGREEMENT, entered into as of this ______ day of _______, 20___, between __________ (hereinafter referred to as the "Publisher"), located at ______________________________, and ____ (hereinafter referred to as the "Author"), located at ____.

WHEREAS, the Author wishes to create a book on the subject of _______________ (hereinafter referred to as the "Work")

WHEREAS, the Publisher is familiar with the work of the Author and wishes to publish a book by the Author; and

WHEREAS, the parties wish to have said publication performed subject to the mutual obligations, covenants, and conditions herein.

NOW, THEREFORE, in consideration of the foregoing premises and the mutual covenants hereinafter set forth and other valuable considerations, the parties hereto agree as follows:

1. **Grant of Rights.** The Author grants, conveys, and transfers to the Publisher in that unpublished Work titled ____, certain limited, exclusive rights as follows:
   (A) To publish, distribute, and sell the Work in the form of a __________________ book;
   (B) In the territory of ____;
   (C) In the______________________ language; and **(D)** For a term of ___________ years.
2. **Reservation of Rights.** All rights not specifically granted to the Publisher are reserved to the Author, including but not limited to electronic rights which are defined as rights in the digitized form of works that can be encoded, stored, and retrieved from such media as computer disks, CD-ROM, computer databases, and network servers.
3. **Delivery of Manuscript.** On or before the ________ day of ___________, 20______, the Author shall deliver to the Publisher a complete manuscript of approximately _______ words, which shall be reasonably satisfactory in form and content to the Publisher and in conformity with any outline or description attached hereto and made part hereof. The manuscript shall be in the following form: [ ] double-spaced hard copy [ ] computer files (specify format ____________________). The manuscript shall include the additional materials listed in Paragraph 4 (except that if an index is to be provided by the Author, it shall be delivered to the Publisher within thirty days of Author's receipt of paginated galleys). If the Author fails to deliver the complete manuscript within ninety days after receiving notice from the Publisher of failure to deliver on time, the Publisher shall have the right to terminate this Agreement and receive back from the Author all monies advanced to the Author pursuant to Paragraphs 4, 5, and 9. If the Author delivers a manuscript which, after being given detailed instructions for revisions by the Publisher and _____ days to complete such revisions, is not reasonably acceptable to the Publisher, then monies advanced to the Author pursuant to Paragraphs 4, 5, and 9 shall be [ ] retained by the Author [ ] repaid to the Publisher [ ] repaid to the Publisher only in the event the Author subsequently signs a contract with another Publisher for the Work.
4. **Additional Materials.** The following materials shall be provided by the Author ____________ ____. The cost of providing these additional materials shall be borne by the Author, provided, however, that the Publisher at the time of signing this Agreement shall give a nonrefundable payment of $_____________ to assist the Author in defraying these costs, which payment shall not be deemed an advance to the Author and shall not be recouped as such.
5. **Permissions.** The Author agrees to obtain all permissions that are necessary for the use of materials copyrighted by others. The cost of providing these permissions shall be borne by the Author, provided, however, that the Publisher at the time of signing this Agreement shall give a nonrefundable payment of $_______ to assist the Author in defraying these costs, which

payment shall not be deemed an advance to the Author and shall not be recouped as such. Permissions shall be obtained in writing and copies shall be provided to the Publisher when the manuscript is delivered.

6. **Duty to Publish.** The Publisher shall publish the Work within ____________ months of the delivery of the complete manuscript. Failure to so publish shall give the Author the right to terminate this Agreement ninety days after giving written notice to the Publisher of the failure to make timely publication. In the event of such termination, the Author shall have no obligation to return monies received pursuant to Paragraphs 4, 5, and 9.
7. **Royalties.** The Publisher shall pay the Author the following royalties: ____ percent of the suggested retail price on the first 5,000 copies sold; ____ percent of the suggested retail price on the next 5,000 copies sold; and ____ percent of the suggested retail price on all copies sold thereafter. These royalty rates shall be discounted only in the following circumstances: ______
____
____

   All copies sold shall be cumulated for purposes of escalations in the royalty rates, including revised editions, except for editions in a different form (such as a paperback reprint of a hardcover original) which shall be cumulated separately. Copies sold shall be reduced by copies returned in the same royalty category in which the copies were originally reported as sold.

   In the event the Publisher has the right pursuant to Paragraph 1(A) to publish the Work in more than one form, the royalty rates specified above shall apply to publication in the form of a ______________ book and the royalty rates for other forms shall be specified here: ______
____
____
____

8. **Subsidiary Rights.** The following subsidiary rights may be licensed by the party indicated and the proceeds divided as specified herein:

Subsidiary Right	Right to License		Division of Proceeds	
	Author	Publisher	Author	Publisher

   If the division of proceeds for any subsidiary right changes after the sale of a certain number of copies, indicate which right, the number of copies required to be sold, and the new division of proceeds ____
____
____

   The Publisher shall have no rights pursuant to this Paragraph 8 if Publisher is in default of any of its obligations under this Agreement. The right to license any subsidiary right not set forth in this Paragraph is retained by the Author. Licensing income shall be divided as specified herein without any reductions for expenses.

   Licensing income shall be collected by the party authorized to license the right and the appropriate percentage remitted by that party to the other party within ten days of receipt. Copies of all licenses shall be provided to both parties immediately upon receipt.
9. **Advances.** The Publisher shall, at the time of signing this Agreement, pay to the Author a nonrefundable advance of $_________, which advance shall be recouped by the Publisher from payments due to the Author pursuant to Paragraph 11 of this Agreement.

10. **Accountings.** Commencing as of the date of publication, the Publisher shall report every ____ months to the Author, showing for that period and cumulatively to date the number of copies printed and bound, the number of copies sold and returned for each royalty rate, the number of copies distributed free for publicity purposes, the number of copies remaindered, destroyed, or lost, the royalties paid to and owed to the Author, and licensing income. If the Publisher sets up a reserve against returns of books, the reserve may only be set up for the four accounting periods following the first publication of the Work and shall in no event exceed 15 percent of royalties due to the Author in any period.
11. **Payments.** The Publisher shall pay the Author all monies due Author pursuant to Paragraph 10 within thirty days of the close of each accounting period.
12. **Right of Inspection.** The Author shall, upon the giving of written notice, have the right to inspect the Publisher's books of account to verify the accountings. If errors in any such accounting are found to be to the Author's disadvantage and represent more than 5 percent of the payment to the Author pursuant to the said accounting, the cost of inspection shall be paid by the Publisher.
13. **Copyright and Authorship Credit.** The Publisher shall, as an express condition of receiving the grant of rights specified in Paragraph 1, take the necessary steps to register the copyright on behalf of the Author and in the Author's name and shall place copyright notice in the Author's name on all copies of the Work. The Author shall receive authorship credit as follows: ________________________________.
14. **Warranty and Indemnity.** The Author warrants and represents that he or she is the sole creator of the Work and owns all rights granted under this Agreement, that the Work is an original creation and has not previously been published (except for those materials for which permissions have been obtained pursuant to Paragraph 5), that the Work does not infringe any other person's copyrights or rights of literary property, nor, to his or her knowledge, does it violate the rights of privacy of, or libel, other persons. The Author agrees to indemnify the Publisher against any final judgment for damages (after all appeals have been exhausted) in any lawsuit based on an actual breach of the foregoing warranties. In addition, the Author shall pay the Publisher's reasonable costs and attorney's fees incurred in defending such a lawsuit, unless the Author chooses to retain his or her own attorney to defend such lawsuit. The Author makes no warranties and shall have no obligation to indemnify the Publisher with respect to materials inserted in the Work at the Publisher's request. Notwithstanding any of the foregoing, in no event shall the Author's liability under this Paragraph exceed $________ or ________ percent of sums payable to the Author under this Agreement, whichever is the lesser. In the event a lawsuit is brought which may result in the Author having breached his or her warranties under this Paragraph, the Publisher shall have the right to withhold and place in an escrow account ______ percent of sums payable to the Author pursuant to Paragraph 11, but in no event may said withholding exceed the damages alleged in the complaint.
15. **Artistic Control.** The Author and Publisher shall consult with one another with respect to the title of the Work, the price of the Work, the method and means of advertising and selling the Work, the number and destination of free copies, the number of copies to be printed, the method of printing and other publishing processes, the exact date of publication, the form, style, size, type, paper to be used, and like details, how long the plates or film shall be preserved and when they shall be destroyed, and when new printings of the Work shall be made. In the event of disagreement after consultation, the Publisher shall have final power of decision over all the foregoing matters except the following, which shall be controlled by the Author____ ____. No changes shall be made in the complete manuscript of the Work by persons other than the Author, except for reasonable copy editing, unless the Author consents to such changes. Publisher shall provide the

Author with galleys and proofs which the Author shall review and return to the Publisher within thirty (30) days of receipt. If the cost of the Author's alterations (other than for typesetting errors or unavoidable updating) exceeds _____ percent of the cost of the typography, the Publisher shall have the right to deduct such excess from royalties due Author hereunder.

16. **Original Materials.** Within thirty days after publication, the Publisher shall return the original manuscript and all additional materials to the Author. The Publisher shall provide the Author with a copy of the page proofs, if the Author requests them prior to the date of publication.
17. **Free Copies.** The Author shall receive ____ free copies of the Work as published, after which the Author shall have the right to purchase additional copies at a ____ percent discount from the retail price.
18. **Revisions.** The Author agrees to revise the Work on request by the Publisher. If the Author cannot revise the Work or refuses to do so absent good cause, the Publisher shall have the right to have the Work revised by a person competent to do so and shall charge the costs of said revision against payments due the Author under Paragraph 11 for such revised edition. In no event shall such revision costs exceed $ ________.
19. **Successors and Assigns.** This Agreement may not be assigned by either party without the written consent of the other party hereto. The Author, however, shall retain the right to assign payments due hereunder without obtaining the Publisher's consent. This Agreement shall be binding on the parties and their respective heirs, administrators, successors, and assigns.
20. **Infringement.** In the event of an infringement of the rights granted under this Agreement to the Publisher, the Publisher and the Author shall have the right to sue jointly for the infringement and, after deducting the expenses of bringing suit, to share equally in any recovery. If either party chooses not to join in the suit, the other party may proceed and, after deducting all the expenses of bringing the suit, any recovery shall be shared equally between the parties.
21. **Termination.** The Author shall have the right to terminate this Agreement by written notice if: **(A)** the Work goes out-of-print and the Publisher, within ninety days of receiving notice from the Author that the Work is out-of-print, does not place the Work in print again. A work shall be deemed out-of-print if the work is not available for sale in reasonable quantities in normal trade channels; **(B)** if the Publisher fails to provide statements of account pursuant to Paragraph 10; **(C)** if the Publisher fails to make payments pursuant to Paragraphs 4, 5, 9, or 11; or **(D)** if the Publisher fails to publish in a timely manner pursuant to Paragraph 6. The Publisher shall have the right to terminate this Agreement as provided in Paragraph 3. This Agreement shall automatically terminate in the event of the Publisher's insolvency, bankruptcy, or assignment of assets for the benefit of creditors. In the event of termination of the Agreement, the Publisher shall grant, convey, and transfer all rights in the Work back to the Author.
22. **Production Materials and Unbound Copies.** Upon any termination, the Author may, within sixty days of notification of such termination, purchase the plates, offset negatives, or computer drive tapes (if any) at their scrap value and any remaining copies at the lesser of cost or remainder value.
23. **Promotion.** The Author consents to the use of his or her name, portrait, or picture for promotion and advertising of the Work, provided such use is dignified and consistent with the Author's reputation.
24. **Arbitration.** All disputes arising under this Agreement shall be submitted to binding arbitration before ____________________________ in the following location ____________________ and shall be settled in accordance with the rules of the American Arbitration Association. Judgment upon the arbitration award may be entered in any court having jurisdiction thereof.
25. **Notice.** Where written notice is required hereunder, it may be given by use of first class mail addressed to the Author or Publisher at the addresses given at the beginning of this Agreement

and shall be deemed received five days after mailing. Said addresses for notice may be changed by giving written notice of any new address to the other party.

26. **Entire Agreement and Modifications.** This Agreement represents the entire Agreement between the parties. All modifications of this Agreement must be in writing and signed by both parties.

27. **Waivers and Defaults.** Any waiver of a breach or default hereunder shall not be deemed a waiver of a subsequent breach or default of either the same provision or any other provision of this Agreement.

28. **Governing Law.** This Agreement shall be governed by the laws of ___________________ State.

IN WITNESS WHEREOF, the parties have signed this Agreement as of the date first set forth above.

Author________________________ Publisher_____________________________
Company Name

By_____________________________
Authorized Signatory, Title

CHAPTER SIXTEEN

The Collaboration Agreement

The first issue to be resolved is how the copyright in the collaboration will be owned.

➢ Tad Crawford, *Business and Legal Forms for Authors and Self-Publishers* (Allworth Press, 2015)

Will you be collaborating with someone else on a book? Have you been asked to ghostwrite a book? Are you a person with ideas who is looking for an experienced writer to get your thoughts down on paper? There are many different kinds of collaborations and the agreements must be in writing if you are to avoid some really sticky problems later on. In every case the details of the agreement should be spelled out. For example, the names of the parties and the names of their agents, if any, should be stated. The nature or subject of the work must be specified, such as autobiography, how-to book, child psychology, cookbook, and so forth. The tentative or working title should be named, and if there is an outline or synopsis of the work, it should be attached to the contract.

Ghostwriting

A ghostwriter is one who writes for and gives credit of authorship to another person. If you are hired to help a person write his autobiography, you may be hired as a ghostwriter. Sometimes specialists in certain fields will hire a ghostwriter to explain esoteric concepts in a way that the lay public will understand. Whether you are hired to ghostwrite or will be contracting with a writer to ghostwrite your book, you need to know all the ramifications.

Before a contract is even considered, both parties should decide on two major issues: the charges and the author credit. *Writer's Market* contains guidelines in these matters. They list "Ghostwriting, as told to" which is writing for a celebrity or expert, and "Ghostwriting, no credit" which could be writing for an individual who is self-publishing, or for a book packager, publisher, agent, or company.

The ghostwriter of the former (as told to) receives a "with" credit line: *John Q. Public with Jane Doe.* This appears on the cover of the book. If a book publisher is involved, the ghost gets the full advance plus 50 percent of royalties. Self-publishers might pay an hourly rate to the writer which could range from $25 to $85, or pay by the page at a rate of $125 to $175 per book page.

A ghostwriter with no credit could expect a rate of anywhere from a low of $5,000 to a high of $50,000 or more, plus expenses. The ghostwriter who is working for a self-publisher should ask for one-fourth down payment, one-fourth when the book is half finished, one-fourth at the three-quarters mark, and the balance upon completion. In both cases, it is wise to charge extra for research, which can be very time-consuming.

According to attorney/author/publisher Tad Crawford, "It is important that the credits accurately reflect what the parties did. The credit could be 'by A and B' or 'story by A and illustrations by B.' 'As told to' indicates one person telling their story to another; while 'with' suggests that one person did some writing and the other person, usually a professional author, shaped and completed the book. It is against public policy for someone to take credit for writing a book which, in fact, was written by someone else."

Equal Partner Collaborations

If it is a joint work and proceeds are equally shared, either party can license the work. Each party's responsibility should be set out in great detail, as well as how they will authorize and share expenses. They also need to decide what will happen if the project is never completed. The issues might be what their individual rights will be in case the book project is never sold. Each author would probably want to retain the right to publish that portion of the book he wrote and be free to publish it by itself or include it in a longer work.

There are so many variables in any collaboration agreement that they can't all be addressed here. But think of all the contingencies you can and detail them in the contract. Some additional points to consider are:

- Specify a date at which time the work should be completed
- Make out a work schedule with sequential deadlines

- State whether the parties will self-publish if they do not receive a publishing contract
- Allow for termination of the contract and state the conditions
- Require that each partner receive a copy of the contract
- Specify which author's name goes first on the book
- Decide what will happen in the event of the death or disability of either party
- Discuss promotion including the use of the parties' names, photos, and bios

More information on collaboration contracts, complete with a CD-ROM containing a form you can modify and print out, can be found in *Business and Legal Forms for Authors and Self-Publishers*. The National Writers Union also provides a guide and a Model Ghostwriting & Collaborations Contract to their members. See Resources in the back of this book for contact information.

Other Contracts and Agreements

Some agreements may be oral contracts where nothing is written down. However, even if your agreement is oral, it is always wise to write a "memo of understanding" where you simply spell out the agreement as you understand it and ask the other party to confirm that this was the way she understood it as well. As an editor and literary consultant, I have signed agreements provided by my clients, such as a nondisclosure agreement. I always agree to that because it puts them at ease. When there were details I wanted to be sure my clients understood, I have prepared a memo of understanding and asked them to sign and date it, indicating that they were in agreement. These memos were mainly to clarify what I would be doing and what my charges would be. For the same project I might charge an hourly rate for some of the work, such as editing, and a flat rate for others, such as page design, news releases, and back-cover writing. It simply made it easier for all of us to keep track—and to keep on track—of how we had chosen to work with each other.

As an author, you may be called upon to sign a lecture contract, an agreement with an independent contractor, or a privacy release. You may need to get permissions from owners of copyrighted materials such as illustrations, photos, paintings, articles, poems, song lyrics, or quotations from books. There are forms for these concerns as well as many more in *Business and Legal Forms*.

CHAPTER SEVENTEEN

Getting Published

I'll publish, right or wrong:
Fools are my theme, let satire be my song
➤ Lord Byron

Authors have more choices than ever before in getting their books published. They range from publishing your book entirely by yourself, using the services of certain specialists to help you through the process, or copublishing with an established publisher, to signing over your publishing rights to a traditional book publisher.

Self-publishing requires an entire chapter by itself. It can be complicated and there have been many changes in the self-publishing world. Copublishing with an established book publisher requires the advice of an experienced attorney in that field. It can be a difficult collaboration and you will want to be sure that you are protected from any unpleasant surprises.

In this chapter I want to concentrate on being published by a traditional book publisher. It will help ease the way if you understand the process and the responsibilities both you and the publisher need to fulfill. And, as in most agreements, there are advantages as well as disadvantages.

Advantages: Not only will it cost you nothing, you probably will get an advance. The publisher will pay for printing, editing, promotion, distribution, and so forth. The general perception among bookstores and book buyers is that a book published by an established publisher is more professional and of a higher quality than a self-published book.

Disadvantages: The author loses much of the control. Income from royalties could be less than the author's potential profit from a self-published book. It could take eighteen months to two years for the publisher to get the book out.

Selling your book to a publisher doesn't mean that you can just sit back and wait until the royalties start rolling in. You still have responsibilities.

Once your book is accepted by a publisher, you become partners. You supply the materials, the publisher supplies the capital, and together you produce a product. Of course, it's not that cold or that simple. It is a business relationship, however. It is—or should be—a relationship of trust, cooperation, and mutual respect. You share a common goal, that of creating a high-quality, commercially viable product you both can be proud of.

Even when you realize that you are involved in a business partnership, it is hard to remove yourself emotionally from that book you created. If you are like most authors, your blood, sweat, tears, and a huge amount of your time went into the production of your manuscript. It is more than an inanimate object to you. It is part of your heart and mind. It may be hard to accept anyone changing that piece of yourself. Yet, you must.

There can also be misunderstandings between author and publisher because it is rare for someone else to see things exactly the way you see them. It will be easier to see the big picture if you know what to expect once you sign the publication agreement. You will find the process more enjoyable if you are able to accept the following.

1. You are not your publisher's only author and possibly not even his favorite.
2. You may have to make compromises that could tear at your heart.
3. Some of your favorite passages may be taken out.
4. You may be required to write a few more chapters.
5. It will seem to take forever before your book appears in bookstores.
6. You must be patient.

There are many things to consider and, although you may share your opinions with the publisher, he is the one who must make most of the decisions. He will be the one to choose the size of the book, whether to publish it in hard cover or paperback, and what to charge for it. But before it even gets to the point of printing and binding, it will go through many processes, and that takes time.

The Author's Responsibility

It is of the utmost importance that you meet the publisher's deadlines. If you do not get all the necessary materials and information to him on time, it could delay the release date of your book.

Among your responsibilities are the following:

1. To edit your work carefully, checking for punctuation, spelling, and grammatical errors.
2. To be accurate, check your facts and, whenever possible, furnish your sources.
3. To avoid any possibility of plagiarism or defamation of character in your writing. You could jeopardize not only your own reputation but your publisher's, too.
4. To be professional at all times. Keep your personal problems to yourself.
5. To be fair and open-minded. Try to see the publisher's viewpoint.

You will probably be expected to provide both a printed copy and a CD or flash drive of your manuscript. Most people now have computers and inkjet or laser printers. If you don't, you may have to get someone with a computer setup to put your manuscript into a Word file, print it out, and save it to a disk for sending to your publisher. Your publisher may ask you to use their "house style" in preparing your manuscript. If he doesn't, you could use the following guidelines furnished by Allworth Press. They are in accordance with the current standard in the industry.

MANUSCRIPT STYLE GUIDELINES FOR AUTHORS

The Manuscript

Please provide a file and a hard copy of the manuscript. The file must be saved in a standard format (recent versions of Microsoft Word or as a rich text format [.rtf] file). If this is a difficulty, *please call to ensure that we will be able to read the files.* Any editorial or style questions can be directed to your editor.

The manuscript should be complete. Information, including bibliographic information and appendixes, should not be left incomplete, unless clearly marked on the pages. With regard to the formatting of the manuscript files, please note the following:

- If you are new to computers, please ask someone to show you how simple it is to use word wrap—that is, allowing the word processing program to wrap your words through to the next line without interruption. Do not use the computer as a typewriter and put carriage returns after each line.
- Manuscripts should be double-spaced with one-inch margins. Do not use condensed type or any special typefaces. *Always* use Times New Roman (or Times or Times Roman), because these fonts seem to translate cross platform fluidly (i.e. from your Mac to our PC; from our PC to the designer's page layout software). Other fonts often cause proofreading nightmares due to translation problems (hyphens become = signs, quotes become capital *A*'s and @ marks, and so on).
- Do not create complex style sheets in Word—in fact, we much prefer it if you do not work with style sheets at all. Use one style—12 point Times New Roman type,

double spaced, justified left, rag right—throughout. If you need to style your heads bold, or you want to add italic for emphasis, or you need to put text in a block, etc.,—please do these things *manually*, not through style sheets.

- Justify text to the left margin only.
- The fewer commands in the file, the better. In the running text, do not underline for emphasis; do not bold (except for heads and subheads); do not capitalize entire words. You can use italic.
- Do not put more than one space between sentences.
- Do not add an extra line space between paragraphs. Indent paragraphs instead, except as described in the bullet point below.
- Do not indent the first paragraph of a chapter, or the first paragraph below a subhead; these should all be flush left.
- The title of the chapter should be flush left, in bold, and include the number of the chapter. A chapter title looks like this:

Chapter 6: Principles of Business Automation

- Subheads are the titles that divide a chapter into parts. They are hierarchical. So for example, if the chapter title is Chapter 6: Principles of Business Automation, the first subhead is Coping with the Photographers Lifestyle. We call that an A head, because it is the first (hierarchical) level of heads below the chapter title. But underneath that there are a number of B heads. They are Hiring Help Won't Always Do and A New Way to Think about Using Computers and A Business Automation Solution. All of these topics fall within the subject area described by the A head, so they are subsidiary to it, and all are B heads. Almost all nonfiction books have some division of material within chapters, so most of them will have A heads. Not all books will need further levels of heads—it is up to you to make that decision.
- Here is how you should designate heads. To indicate which is which, heads need to be labeled and lightly styled, as follows. *A*-heads should be consistently bold flush left, and *B*-heads should be consistently bold indented. If you have C subsubsubheads, they should be indented and styled as bold italic: Labeling the level of the head is more important than styling it.

The Main Chapter Title

Use a subhead for each new subject. In addition each subhead should be indicated like this:

A Lovely A Subhead

Then you should have running text below the A head, before you have a B head, because we don't like to have heads directly below heads.

Or If You Need a B Subsubhead

Blah, blah, blah, more running text . . . until perhaps you find you need another level of heads in which case you would have to resort to using a C subsubsubhead, which looks like this.

This would be the c head

Continue with the running text.

Please remember *it is not your job to design the mansucript on your computer*, but it is your job to set up the structure of the manuscript clearly so that others can create a design. If you have any question about what subheads are and how to use the subheads, please call and speak to us.

A subhead should occur about every two hundred words (roughly once per double-spaced page).

- Add a line space before subheads.
- As regards sidebars (more about this below), bulleted and numbered lists, forms inserted into the text, in short anything that interrupts the regular running text, make sure that you mark it clearly again using the **[square brackets]** method denoted above in the section on subheads. So for example, at the beginning of a special form inserted into the running text, you would type **[begin form]** and at the end you would type **[end form]**. Or if, for example, you have boxed text, you can mark it **[begin boxed text]** before and **[end boxed text]** at the end.
- Use the spellcheck function on all text.

Use of Images

If your book is going to contain illustrated materials (i.e. photographs, charts, graphs, and so on), you should let us know how many there are and where these items will need to be placed. We will accept images in multiple formats (digital, black and white prints, transparencies, etc.), but please let us know in advance what formats you plan to use. If you are using digital images, our printer has specifications as to file size, resolution, and type of file. We can work with JPEGs, TIFFs, EPSs, PDFs, but it's important that the image have enough resolution for print. This generally means that the image has to be 300 dpi, at printed size. If you are using digital images, *note that the image files should not be embedded in the text.* Digital images need to be sent to us on a separate disk. Make sure that you number all images and that the number corresponds to

1. a numbered caption, if one is necessary
2. a place marker in the text.

For example, if you are using slides in your book, you should number the slides 1, 2, 3, 4, etc. Then, in the text at the appropriate place you should insert the marker **[insert slide 1 here]** When the typesetter goes through the file, he will be able to substitute the correct image for the correct place marker.

If you are using digital files, please make sure that the file name corresponds to the place marker in the text. If your file is called girl2.tif, make sure that the place marker in the file says **[insert girl2.tif].**

It is extremely important that pictures are named or numbered and that the system of naming or numbering is *exactly* the same on the picture or file *and* in the text. Remember, the typesetter is not familiar with your book, and he is not going to be able to figure out which images go where without very specific guidance from you.

One other issue affects pictures, which doesn't really belong here, because it's not about style, but is very important. If you are using images, make sure that you have the *right* to use those images. For example, if you resolve to use a full page illustration by a prominent living artist without getting his permission, you are making a very bad decision. If you want to use a photograph you took of a model, and she never signed a release, better contact her now and get her to sign that release. Permissions can be sticky; call if you have questions and we will offer guidance.

Style

Matters of style should, for the most part, follow *The Chicago Manual of Style,* 16th edition and *Webster's Collegiate Dictionary,* 11th edition. Be consistent in all matters of style and spelling. Make a style sheet in which you resolve all questions of style and spelling, such as names (which should be fact-checked) or words that are not in the dictionary (e.g., technical terms or terminology particular to your subject). Turn in this style sheet with the manuscript so we can benefit from it.

Keep to the agreed-upon page count for the book. Please ask any questions you may have, since the ultimate production of the book will be greatly aided by following these guidelines.

Some General Matters of Style

- Paragraphs should rarely run longer than half a page.
- Make sure that the table of contents matches the text. Often the chapter titles appear one way in the contents and another in the chapter itself (the same goes for subheads).
- Always use the serial comma—that is, for items in a series, always put a comma after the last item before "and" or "or" (e.g., A, B, and C).
- Em dashes should have no spaces on either side (e.g., fish—small, medium, and large). If you have not created a shortcut key in order to insert em dashes, please use a double dash—which will convert easily to a proper em dash.
- There is no space before or after a forward slash.
- Watch for which/that confusion.
- Watch for noun/pronoun agreement (e.g., do not refer to a company as "them" or use "they" when referring to one person). In regard to gender, try to alternate examples from paragraph to paragraph or from case to case (it is often a good idea to assign genders to particular hypothetical examples and use them consistently throughout the manuscript—"the musician" is consistently referred to as "he," "the lawyer" is consistently referred to as "she," and so on).

Incorrect Pronoun Agreement with Antecedent

The desire to be politically correct and gender sensitive has led to appalling grammatical transgressions. Witness this worst of all possible scenarios:

> *Then if a person signs he/she would be perjuring himself if they did not have such authority.*

The problem is of course, that "a person" is not gender specific, and in an effort to maintain gender neutrality the author starts out with the construct "he/she." This would be grammatically okay, although it is awkward. (And it is not part of Allworth's "house style," so we would probably change it.) Once "he/she" has been established, however, one must follow through with it. Starting with that construct, the sentence would have to read:

> *Then if a person signs he/she would be perjuring him/herself if he/she did not have such authority.*

Very inelegant, and leads to much repetition of either/or pronouns, if we continue to have more sentences about "a person."

If one wants to follow through with the gender implied by the use of the word "himself"; the whole sentence has to be masculine. Thus:

> *Then if a person signs he would be perjuring himself if he did not have such authority.*

Actually, that is very clean; and probably would be my choice—radical feminism be damned. Although I would probably make the next "a person" in another example in the book into a female. As in:

> *If a person had the good sense not to sign, she would avoid perjuring herself if she did not have such authority.*

And how about the use of "they"? Although "they" is commonly used in spoken language, in connection with nongender specific nouns, it is a plural pronoun, and really should only be used like this:

> *Then if people sign they would be perjuring themselves if they did not have such authority.*

The plural pronoun must have a plural antecedent.

But what about this tricky construct? Doesn't it circumvent the gender bias problems?

> *Then if a person signs, he or she would be perjuring themselves if they did not have such authority.*

Sorry, the conjunction between "he or she" does not allow you to switch to plural pronouns in midstream. This would have to be corrected to:

> *Then if a person signs he or she would be perjuring himself or herself if he or she did not have such authority.*

- Always spell out the word "and" in running text (and even in bulleted lists), unless it is the case that an ampersand (&) appears as a part of a company's legitimate name.
- Spell out the word "versus" unless citing a legal case.
- The words "street," "avenue," "boulevard," or "suite" should be spelled out in addresses.

Chapters and Subheads

- Chapter titles and all levels of subheads should be in title case (i.e., have initial letters of each word capitalized, except for articles, prepositions, and connectives). The first letter of the first and last word should always be capitalized.
- Don't start chapters with subheads. The first subhead should always follow a block of text introducing the chapter.
- When referring to another chapter in the book, use numerals for the chapter numbers and do not capitalize the word "chapter" (e.g., see chapter 14). The same goes for appendixes (e.g., appendix B). Cross-references between chapters should be filled in when the manuscript is handed in.

Lists and Text Boxes

- Use text boxes sparingly, if necessary. Usually, material can be organized by separating it into paragraphs dividing it with A- or B-heads. Stories, examples, checklists,

and forms lend themselves to boxes and "sidebars." These should not be less than seventy-five words or more than a book page and never more than a two-page spread.
- If you wish to box certain text, indicate this in the manuscript by typing **[begin box]** at the start of the box, and **[end box]** where it concludes. Text in a box should be able to stand by itself and should not be fixed as to where it falls in the chapter.
- Avoid long lists.
- For short lists, use bullets—but try not to do so often. A short bulleted list is often better run together as a paragraph.
- Only number lists if the numbering makes the list easier to understand (such as with a series of steps to be taken). If you are numbering, do not then use lettering for a later list.
- The first letter of a list item is always capitalized, even if the list is a grammatical continuation of the introductory sentence.
- If the reader might want to check off items, it is possible to make checklists by using boxes that can be checked rather than bullets.

Italics versus Quotation Marks

- In addition to specific matters of emphasis, italics are used for: titles of books, periodicals, works of art, long poems and musical compositions, titles of exhibitions, and foreign words or phrases not in the dictionary.
- "Words as words" (e.g., definitions) are set in quotation marks.
- "Letters as letters" are set in italics (e.g., the letter *r*).
- If a periodical or newspaper title begins with the word "the," it should not be capitalized or set in italics (e.g., the *New York Times,* the *New Yorker*).
- Books, films, and works of art with titles beginning with the word "the" should be set in all italics and title case (e.g., *The Artist's Guide to New Markets*).
- Articles published in periodicals are set in quotation marks.
- Do not use the words "so-called" before words in quotation marks.

Numbers

- Numbers one to one hundred should be spelled out.
- Ages are spelled out (sixty-five years old).
- Use numerals for percentages in running text, with the word "percent" spelled out (75 percent)
- Amounts in dollars should be left in numerals with the dollar sign in front ($25.00, or simply $25). This applies to other currency as well (£50, or ¥1,000).
- Always use a comma with numerals unless otherwise instructed (e.g., shutter speeds of camera equipment are typically left without commas).

Dialogue

- Interior, unspoken, or imagined dialogue is not set in quotation marks, unless to avoid confusion. This is also the case for maxims, proverbs, and familiar expressions.
- When a quotation runs over the course of more than one paragraph and the speaker remains the same, quotation marks are placed at the beginning, but not at the end, of each paragraph, and then at the end of the quote.
- When there is a quotation within a quotation, use single quotes.

Spelling

The following words should be spelled and capitalized as follows:

- Internet
- website
- email
- zine
- online/offline

The Index

By contract, you are required to provide us with an index for your book. Although many word processing programs have an indexing option, unfortunately, you will not be able to use this to create your index. Rather, you will have to wait until the book is designed and in galley pages, and then provide a separate, alphabetized file, containing the indexed topics, and the page numbers as listed in the galleys. If you are new to indexing, *The Chicago Manual of Style* provides detailed instructions as to how to index in Chapter 17. If you choose not to provide an index (many authors do not), we will outsource the galleys to a professional indexer, and that charge will be held against your royalties.

Fact Checking

We do not have a fact-checking department. Although our copyeditors and proofreaders do a valiant job of double-checking, you are ultimately responsible for making sure that dates are correct, names and foreign words are spelled correctly, images are properly captioned, credited, cropped, and aligned, and so on.

The Publisher's Responsibility

1. To provide qualified editing and guidance
2. To produce a professional-quality book
3. To publish your book when promised
4. To listen to and value your point of view
5. To pay your advance and royalties in a timely manner

Many of these issues will have been addressed in the agreement you signed with your publisher.

The Publishing Process

There are good reasons that it takes so long between the signing of the publishing agreement and the time your book actually appears in bookstores. Your manuscript goes through many hands before it turns into a book. In a large publishing house, it can go through an acquisition editor, a development editor, a copy editor, a designer, and one or more proofreaders. Small book publishers may have only one editor.

The following are some of the steps involved in the process of producing a bound book.

1. The manuscript goes to the copy editor.
2. The edited manuscript is returned to the author for her review of the changes and, if necessary, for supplying additional copy.
3. The book cover is designed and approved.
4. The book's interior is designed and sample pages are typeset.
5. The page design is reviewed.
6. When all the edits have been made and the design has been approved, the final typesetting is done.
7. A set of proofs of the typeset book is sent to the author for review.
8. Any needed corrections are done and the final pages are sent to the printer.
9. The printer submits "bluelines" or proofs to the publisher for final approval.
10. The printed pages are bound into a book.

All along the way, there are decisions and choices to be made. In a large publishing company, these decisions are often made in committee. Small publishers will have fewer people evaluating the content and design of the book and can often get a book into print faster than a major publisher.

CHAPTER EIGHTEEN

Self-Publishing

A person who publishes a book willfully appears before the populace with his pants down. . . . If it is a good book nothing can hurt him. If it is a bad book nothing can help him.

➤ Edna St. Vincent Millay

In the past five years self-publishing has changed dramatically. Companies that are set up to help authors publish their books themselves have popped up everywhere. They provide services that cover the entire process—from editing your manuscript, formatting the interior of the book (both paper books and ebooks), and designing the cover, to sales, promotion, and distribution. Some of these companies do a very good job but many of them are inexperienced and incapable of putting out a professional-looking book. It's a minefield out there, with hidden hazards everywhere. I don't want to alarm you but I do want you to be careful.

Printing costs are no longer a major concern. There are print-on-demand (POD) companies that will print just one book at a time and sometimes at the point of purchase. If you want to have a few books on hand for sending to reviewers, giving to friends or clients, or selling at a promotional event, you can now have as few as twenty-five copies of your book printed digitally at most printers that specialize in books. A minimum run of 1,000 used to be the case when offset printers were the only choice and, even though the cost per book was less, the total bill would be several thousand dollars.

You don't have to print your book. You can sell it as an ebook that buyers can download over the Internet. In the future more and more books will be digitized and read on electronic book readers, e-readers for short. Even as printed paper media is shrinking, electronic media is expanding.

If you have the time, the talent, and the knowledge to do most of it yourself, you might make more money publishing your own book than you would with a traditional publisher. Authors with a publishing contract generally get from 5 percent to 15 percent of the cover price in royalties. Advances from publishers can range from $100 to $5,000 or more. Your advance can be much higher if you have a track record of selling over 10,000 books during the first few months after it is published.

It used to be that having your book published by an established publisher was an indication that your book was of professional quality. Self-published books did not have a very good reputation. But over the past few years that has changed. Some of them are big sellers and, even after their costs to produce, they are profitable to their author/publisher. No middleman means more money for the author.

Authors whose agent got them the deal with publishers have to give the agent 15 percent of their royalties, and that cuts into their profit. In fact, their royalty statement goes to the agent first who takes his or her cut out of it and sends the author what is left.

As both the publisher and the author, however, *you* are the one who will have to put in most of the money up front. You are the one who is taking the risk. But if you put out a high quality book that is well-written and professionally edited and if it is on a subject that interests a lot of readers, and if you do a good job of marketing and promotion, you just might make your book a bestseller. Yes, there are quite a few *ifs,* but there are opportunities now that you never had before. There is so much you can do without having to spend a fortune.

Many people have self-published, learning how to write, edit, produce, promote, and market their books themselves. Among my clients are authors who are producing books with no plans to take it to a traditional publisher. They already know where and how to sell them. Some have already done so. One of these entrepreneurs is an English teacher who wrote a book about the various fields of writing with an explanation of what is involved in each one. He self-published it with a print run of 5,000 and sold out his first edition within a year or so, marketing it to home schooling programs.

Another successful self-publisher was a woman who wrote a weekly column in the form of questions and answers on homeowner associations for a newspaper. She put her articles into a book and sold the book to condominium and cooperative associations as well as to individuals who live in such communities. She sold all 12,000 copies of her first edition within two years.

The owner of an "angel store," a retail gift shop that specializes in all kinds of objects having to do with angels from knick-knacks and jewelry to paintings and books, decided to write and publish his own book. He ordered a print run of 5,000 and, selling out within two years, printed a revised edition and had twice the number of books printed because he knew he would eventually sell them all. They were sold not only in his own store but in angel stores throughout the world.

Many authors have done very well with their self-published books. The key is in knowing where you can sell them. A married couple I know sold their house and bought a motor home when they retired. They had always loved to travel and decided to spend the autumn years of their lives "on the road." Never having enjoyed packing and unpacking, staying in hotels and eating out every night, they found a way to travel without ever having to leave their home. They knew the best and least expensive places to park their motor home overnight. They had found out where the most interesting places were and how to get there. They kept descriptive travelogue journals of their experiences and made notes of special sites. Eventually, they began producing guides to attractions along specific routes and began publishing a series of books which they sold in gift shops along highways, gas stations, out-of-the-way bookstores, and by mail from their website. After a while their books started paying for their trips.

Dan Poynter, who has written the definitive book on self-publishing, "fell into publishing," he says. He wrote a technical treatise on the parachute and, unable to get a publisher interested, he went directly to a printer. When the orders poured in, he became a publisher. In 1973 he wrote and published a book on hang gliding and sold over 130,000 copies.

Many authors publish their own books even if they plan to find a publisher for it later. Very often it is easier to convince a publisher to take your book once they see it in book form and know that you have already sold a number of copies.

The first edition of *Author's Toolkit* was self-published. That was in 2000, right at the turn of the millennium. I had been editing as a freelancer for a few years by then, helping authors get their books ready for publication and I kept notes on the questions they asked, the mistakes they made, and the challenges they faced. I started noticing that I had a lot of information in my notes and emails to them, explaining what needed to be done at various phases of the process. The goal was always to help them turn their work into a book that could be published—and look like a professional author had written it.

Over a period of a year I had written enough notes to fill several chapters and I decided it was ready to be turned into a book and be published. I didn't even try to find a publisher for it because there were a lot of books out there on how to write a book. Mine was different, I thought, but still it wasn't likely to get me a publishing contract. So I published it myself. I figured I could sell it in my writing seminars and give it to my editing clients to help them along so that they wouldn't have to spend so much on an editor (me).

I knew it was going to cost a lot to produce. I hired a professional book cover designer, Robert Aulicino, who had been the art director of a major New York book publisher and had designed many bestselling book covers. I did the editing, formatting, and interior design myself, using bestselling books as a model. Then I did what you had to do in those days—I had a thousand books printed, figuring that they would last me about ten years at the rate I expected to sell them (or give to my editing clients). Digital printing wasn't of high quality in those days so I had them printed on offset printers by a company that specialized in books. It was costly but I sold some real estate I had in the mountains to pay for it. It was a big gamble on myself and I thought I was probably being foolish but it was something I wanted to do.

I sent copies of the book out to reviewers and it got good reviews in *Library Journal,* the *Los Angeles Times,* and a few smaller publications. As a result, the books started selling with orders going directly to Baker & Taylor, a wholesaler. That company called me and asked me what was going on. I had tried to get them to handle my book a few weeks before but they had refused, saying they didn't work with self-publishers. With all those orders, though, they wanted me now. I immediately signed on with them and within a few weeks I had sold several hundred books. In less than a year and a half I had sold nearly 4,000. I had to have more books printed along the way. But even with all my expenses, it turned out to be a very good investment.

The glow of owning a publishing company had dimmed considerably by then. I wanted more time to write. I decided I would try to find a "real" publisher for the revised edition of the book. I sent out queries, along with copies of the book and the reviews it had gotten to three traditional book publishers and two of them called me on the phone and offered me a deal. I chose Allworth Press and considered myself very fortunate. My working relationship with Tad Crawford, the publisher of Allworth, has always been excellent and the company has since published three more of my books.

Authors don't have to go to all that expense now to self-publish. And it is still possible to self-publish the first edition of your book and get a contract with a traditional publisher to publish subsequent editions, if that is your goal.

The world of technology is changing rapidly, giving authors a vast array of opportunities they never had before. Along with those opportunities comes the need to access new information and learn more about the entire process of producing a book. It is a lot more work than most of us want to do. But this is the new reality and if we wish to write and get our books published, we need to learn new things all the time.

By the end of 2014, digital books had made great headway into the book business. Ebook sales were growing but not as fast as they had been just a few months earlier. The Bookseller's Digital Census tracks annually how the book business is managing the shift from printed to digital books. The Census was completed by more than 1,000 respondents. Among their findings were the following.

- Digital sales continue to grow and are likely to overtake print by 2025
- Subscriptions are on the rise. Twenty-eight percent of publishers sell subscriptions.
- Self-published authors are happier than traditionally published writers. On a scale of 1 to 10, traditionally published authors rated their level of satisfaction as 5.7 while self-published authors rated their level as 7.1.
- Nearly half of self-published authors have sold fewer than 1,000 ebooks.

- Most respondents think the industry is not as prepared as it should be for the next stage of the digital revolution.

Self-Publishing Companies

There are companies that will take care of all the details of publishing your book for you, for a fee. You can choose from a menu of services that includes editorial evaluation, page set-up, book cover design, and printing. Many authors use these companies with varying degrees of satisfaction. These are not traditional publishers—you pay them to publish under their publishing name. There has been an explosion of companies that will publish a writer's book for a price. In fact, because of the self-publishing revolution, many small traditional publishers are being wiped out.

How do you choose a self-publishing company when there are so many? Well, it is not easy and no one can recommend a particular company to everyone. One size does not fit all. Since they all offer different services at different costs, it's best to check them out yourself. Depending on what you want them to do for you, the costs can range from several hundred dollars to upwards of $25,000. Do a search under "self-publishing companies" and you will be amazed at how much information you will get.

You can choose a size for your book, format it yourself in Word, and turn it into a PDF to send to the company. In some cases you can simply send them the manuscript in Word and the company will format it to fit a certain size page. If you have an idea for the cover art you can send that as well. Their graphic design department will design the cover for you. If you do most of the design and formatting yourself, you could have your book in your hand within a couple of weeks. Since they can print on demand, you can order one copy at a time.

If you think that having one of these companies take over the job of publishing your book means that you will get a professional-looking book, you may be disappointed. While they can put out a book that looks good on the surface, the major concern is their editing of your book. They will make suggestions but if you want professional content guidance and line-by-line copy editing you'd best hire an experienced book editor yourself. Most self-publishing companies' editors don't take the time to work with you personally and you rarely get to discuss the edits.

The greatest telltale sign that a book is self-published is the quality of the editing. Just as an established publisher will turn aside a book that has been poorly edited, you as a self-publisher should be just as picky. Your goal should be to produce a book that is as professional-looking as one from a well-known publisher. Book editing is a specialty, and an English teacher or journalist is not likely to edit your book according to book publishing standards. Be sure you get an editor who follows the style rules of *The Chicago Manual of Style.*

Many bookstores don't want to carry self-published books because they are often inferior to traditionally published books. And they don't want to clog their shelves with books that don't move. Some self-publishing companies can get your books into bookstores but that doesn't mean they will sell. You will still have to do the promotion and marketing. If you choose to have the company do that for you, you will pay dearly for it and there still isn't a guarantee that you will sell enough copies to recoup your costs.

However, even with all the concerns about publishing with such companies, they may be your best choice because they certainly know more about book production than the average person and it will be easier than trying to do everything yourself. And many authors are happy with the process and the result.

You can self-publish without using a company to handle all the details for you. Many authors have done just that. They form their own publishing company to publish and sell their books. It isn't simple but if you take the time, you can learn how to do it.

Setting Up a Publishing Company

You can form a publishing company without having to consult an attorney, although I don't advise it. It's a good idea to have someone knowledgeable look at your plan. Once you have decided on a name for your company you must file a DBA (Doing Business As) form with your county, checking their records to be sure that the name is not already in use. You will then have to publish the DBA in a local newspaper for a period of time. You'll need a sales tax permit to sell your books, which you can get from your state's Board of Equalization. Some cities require a business license. Check with your state's and city's local government offices regarding their requirements. If you have a tax accountant, you should check with him regarding any state and federal tax matters you might need to consider, such as paying taxes on the profits or taking a tax write-off for expenses.

Getting and Filling Out the Publishing Forms

For each book you publish you will need an ISBN (International Standard Book Number). You should also get your copyright registered with the U.S. Copyright Office. You will need an LCCN (Library of Congress Card Number). You should complete an "Advance Book Information" form so that your book will be listed in the databases *Books in Print* and *Forthcoming Books* that provide information to bookstores and libraries. You will also need a bar code if you plan to sell your books through retail establishments such as bookstores and gift shops.

These forms need to be completed and submitted in a specific order. For example, you'll need your ISBN before you apply for your LCCN. The following is a list of the forms with a brief explanation of each one.

Copyright Registration

See Chapter on Copyright Information.

ISBN Publisher Prefix

The International Standard Book Number (ISBN) identifies books and book-like products published internationally. The United States ISBN Agency is the only source authorized to assign ISBNs to publishers located in the United States, U.S. Virgin Islands, Guam, and Puerto Rico. The ISBN establishes and identifies one title from one specific publisher and is unique to that edition. The purpose is to allow for more efficient marketing of products by booksellers, libraries, universities, wholesalers, and distributors.

Each ISBN consists of thirteen digits that are divided into five parts: (1) the current ISBN-13 will be prefixed by "978"; (2) the group or country identifier, which shows a national or geographic grouping of publishers; (3) the publisher identifier which shows a particular publisher within a group; (4) the title identifier of a particular title of edition; and (5) a check digit, the single digit at the end of the ISBN that validates the ISBN.

Once an ISBN number or group of numbers has been assigned to a publisher, the publisher can assign the number to its publications. ISBNs can be purchased online at MyIdentifiers.com/isbn/main, the new home of the U.S. ISBN Agency and Bowker Identifier Services. A self-publisher can now get an ISBN and Barcode package for $55.

Books in Print

When your book is ready to be sold, register it in *Books In Print* at www.bowkerlink.com. *Books In Print* is the main directory that bookstores, online retailers, and libraries use when looking for books for their customers. Registration is free and details are provided at the time ISBNs are emailed to publishers.

Library of Congress Control Number

If you want to participate in the Preassigned Control Number Program, you must complete and submit an Application to Participate. When you are approved, an account number and password will be sent to you via email. Then you will log on to the PCN system and complete a Preassigned Control Number Application. The Library staff will then assign a control number which you will print on the back of the title page (the copyright page) in the following manner:

Library of Congress Control Number: 2010012345.

For more information go to pcn.loc.gov/pcn.

* * *

You, as both author and publisher of your book, make all of the decisions and have control of the entire process. All profits belong to you alone. However, if you are unable to do everything yourself to get your book ready for the printer, you must find qualified people to perform some of the services for you. You, as the publisher, are responsible for all the promotion, distribution, and sales. The process of doing it all yourself may seem daunting but the rewards can be great. You retain complete control and if you sell thousands of books your profit would be greater than doing it any other way.

There are ways to self-publish a book that do not require the services of a printing company or bindery. Following are a few ideas.

Self-publishing a Spiral-bound Book

Advantages: Photocopies can be made and books bound the same day by most photocopying stores. You can purchase a binding machine and bind them yourself as you need them. You can also run off high-quality copies of the pages on your own laser printer. Many cookbooks are spiral bound because the pages lay flat, making it easier for the cook to follow the recipes.

Disadvantages: It can end up costing more than a digital short-run printing company would charge and may not look as professional. Spiral-bound books have no spine on which to put the title of the book and because of that, many bookstores and libraries will not carry them.

Creating a Hand-crafted Book

Advantages: This may be appropriate for art books, poetry, or family history. It can become a work of art in itself or a family heirloom. It is a great creative outlet for authors who are also artists or craftsmen and who enjoy the process of creating the entire product. The pages can be printed on three-hole-punch paper, using a printer with a duplexer (prints on both sides) and put into a three-ring notebook. If there aren't a lot of pages, they can be stapled.

Disadvantages: Depending upon the materials used, it could be quite costly per unit.

Producing an Audio Book

Advantages: You could record it yourself in a quiet room of your home or office, in which case the only costs would be the audiotape or compact discs. It can be "read" by the blind or listened to on long automobile trips. It can be produced in the author's own voice, which would be valuable for family histories and memoirs. Later it could be transcribed and made into a printed book.

Disadvantages: For good sound quality you would need to record it in a professional recording studio with a sound engineer, which could be expensive. Promotion and distribution would be challenging. If you don't have a pleasant voice that records well, you may have to hire a professional actor.

If you decide to produce your book so that it has the look of a professionally published book, you can certainly do so. Hundreds of thousands of authors have self-published. And while most of them have not earned back their costs, many self-publishers have been very successful.

Not all writers' goals are to make a living as a writer or even to earn any money through their writing. Many writers have things they want to write about and maybe even to turn into a book with no desire or expectation of selling it. Some write their memoirs as a self-healing project as well as a family history to leave to their children or grandchildren. Even if your family members don't read it until many years later, someday they will probably want to, and it will be your parting gift to them. Many people want to record their family recipes that have been passed down from generation to generation. Their cookbooks may find a wide readership but even if they don't, most people have parents, aunts, uncles, cousins, children, and grandchildren who would treasure such a book. In some large extended families, this group could account for a hundred or more books.

Printing costs are no longer a major concern since now you can have as few as twenty-five copies of your book printed. When you go with print-on-demand (POD) companies you can have just one book printed at a time and sometimes at the point of purchase, such as a book store. No more ordering more books than you can sell and having to find a place in your garage to store them. In fact, you don't even have to print your book. You can sell it as an ebook that buyers can download over the Internet.

The major expenses you will need to consider are the costs of editing, proofreading, designing the cover and interior of the book, formatting, and printing. You should always have someone proofread the final formatted pages of your book. If you do not require the services of a professional editor and you can do the cover and page design and the computer typesetting yourself, you will save yourself those expenses.

There's no getting around it, there are still costs involved in publishing a book. But now there is help with those expenses: a rapidly growing crowdfunding industry.

Crowdfunding

This is a word that was just recently added to the *Merriam Webster Unabridged* (2014). The crowdfunding industry has grown enormously over the past five years. It is helping people raise billions in funding for everything from donations for art projects to equity financing for businesses. Specialized crowdfunding sites include funding for charity, gaming, real estate, startups, and just about anything you can imagine.

How does it work? There are two basic crowdfunding models. They are (1) **rewards-based crowdfunding** where people can prepurchase products, buy experiences, or simply donate. Although this type of funding might go toward helping a business, the funders aren't allowed to invest or to become shareholders.

The other model (2) is called **equity crowdfunding.** It allows people to become shareholders in a company. There are thousands of companies online that are looking for investors. The companies sell ownership stakes in the form of equity or debt.

Indie authors are increasingly seeking crowdfunding for their book projects. The idea is for authors to have their readers fund their next book directly in exchange for access to the process. They also offer exclusive goodies at various pledge levels.

The following are a few of the rewards-based crowdfunding sites:

Kickstarter is (as of this writing) the leading rewards-based crowdfunding site for creative projects. Tens of thousands of people have pledged millions of dollars to projects involving games, music, film, art, design, and technology. They do not offer equity crowdfunding.

Indiegogo is open to many different kinds of projects. It has a larger international presence than Kickstarter. It was initially formed to fund indie film and theater projects but it now is expanding to cover charities and pet projects.

Crowdrise was formed for donations to charitable causes.

Quirky Quirky is a rewards-based platform as well as an online community used by product inventors and makers. It is also includes collaborating with a crowd in the development of a prototype.

Unbound is a crowdfunding platform for writers. It is also a book publisher. This is how it works: First, the author pitches an idea. Unbound then lets you, the proposed funder, listen to the authors' ideas for what they want to write before they even start. If you like it you can pledge to support it. When there are enough supporters, the author can start writing. The higher your pledge, the greater rewards you'll receive, from your name in the back of the book to lunch with the author. You then gain access to the author's private "shed" to get updates on the book's progress. After the book is written, designed, edited, and printed, Unbound sends it to you either as an ebook or a limited edition hardback or paperback.

Unbound fulfills all the normal publishing functions and splits the book's net profit 50/50 with the author. Of all the books Unbound has published, only one third came from female authors. Knowing that this gender imbalance is widespread across the publishing industry, they recently launched Women in Print to publish interesting, challenging female authors. To find out more about Unbound Crowdfunding go to http://unbound.co.uk/books.

Crowdfunding is relatively new on the scene. This is where your skill at researching can come in handy. There are bound to be a lot of changes in the companies involved and in their processes so be sure to check them out.

Pricing Your Printed Book

Before your book goes to a printer you'll have to decide on a price. Check other books of a similar nature and size to see what they are charging, then price your book within the range those books are selling for. The disadvantages to pricing your book too low are that you may find it hard to recoup your costs per book and you risk having your book being considered worth less than others. The disadvantage to pricing above the market is that it may be passed over for a book with a less expensive price tag.

Pricing Ebooks

There is a lot of confusion about how to price an ebook. But, generally, ebooks are priced lower than printed books for obvious reasons: it costs a lot less to produce an ebook than a printed book. Therefore they should sell them for less. But who decides the price? That's where a major conflict erupted in 2014 between Hatchette (a major publisher) and Amazon. It was settled in November 2014. The details are too complicated to explain here but you can find information about their dispute on the Internet.

Depending on who the publisher and the author are, and what size the book is, an ebook price usually ranges from 99 cents to $7.00. In a recent survey it was found that low pricing gave a book a competitive advantage. Books priced $2.99 and $3.99 on average received four times as many unit sales as those priced at $7.99 and above.

Sending Out Review Copies

It is important to send out review copies to influential journals. A good review in *Library Journal* can generate orders for 1,000 books or more within the first few weeks of publication. Review books should be sent out four to six months before the publication date. Following is a list of some of the reviewers you may wish to send your book to. Be sure to check their website to get information on submitting your book for review. The guidelines are different for each one.

Publishers Weekly
Forecasts
245 W. 17th Street
New York, NY 10011-5300

Library Journal
Book Review Editor
245 W. 17th Street
New York, NY 10011-5300

Kirkus Reviews
Library Advance Information
770 Broadway
New York, NY 10003-9597

ALA Booklist
Up Front, Advance Reviews
50 E. Huron Street
Chicago, IL 60611

New York Times Book Review
229 W. 43rd Street
New York, NY 10036

New York Review of Books
1755 Broadway, Floor 5
New York, NY 10019

New York Times
Daily Book Review Section
229 W. 43rd Street
New York, NY 10036

Los Angeles Times Book Review
202 W. First Street
Los Angeles, CA 90012

School Library Journal
245 W. 17th Street
New York, NY 10011-5300

Choice
Editorial Department
100 Riverview Center
Middletown, CT 06457

Midwest Book Review
278 Orchard Drive
Oregon, WI 53575

Chicago Tribune Books
Book Reviews
435 N. Michigan Ave.
Chicago, IL 60611

Independent Publisher
Jenkins Group
400 W. Front Street, Suite 4A
Traverse City, MI 49684

Newsday
Book Reviews
Two Park Avenue
New York, NY 10016

San Francisco Chronicle
Book Reviews
901 Mission
San Francisco, CA 94103

USA Today
Book Reviews
1000 Wilson Blvd.
Arlington, VA 22229

Washington Post
Book World
1150 15th Street, NW
Washington, DC 10071

And here is a new place to send your book for review: *The New York Journal of Books*, which commenced operations in early 2010. Although they do not accept direct book submissions, they state, "To request a review please email us at www.nyjournalofbooks.com with a brief description of book. Include publisher/publicist contact information. In general, books should be submitted a minimum of four weeks ahead of release."

If you get a good review in one or more of the above publications, be prepared to get a lot of attention. Don't be surprised if a book wholesaler contacts you, the publisher, to place orders of a hundred or more books at a time. In such a case, it will be necessary to sign an agreement with the wholesaler. Many bookstores and libraries will not order directly from a publisher, only through a wholesaler such as Baker & Taylor and Ingram. Major wholesalers expect a discount of 55 percent of the cover price of the book. If you sign with a distributor (from which wholesalers and some bookstores and libraries purchase their books) you will have to give up as much as 65 percent. But it makes sense when you consider that they may be ordering your books by the hundreds or thousands.

Even if you don't get your book reviewed by any of the above, you may be able to get local newspapers, magazines, or periodicals to review your book and write an article about you and your book in their publication. You might be pleasantly surprised at how many books you can sell locally if you also combine this kind of promotion with a book-signing at a neighborhood book store. Small independent bookstores and other shops will often take books penned by local authors on consignment and pay you 60 percent of the cover price when they sell them.

You can also get your book reviewed for a fee. However, the value of a review you have to pay for is questionable.

* * *

There is "A Bright Future for Indie Authors," according to an article in *Publishers Weekly* in November 2014. A number of things have changed in the past few years for self-publishers. Among them are the following.

- Bowker, the official U.S. ISBN agency, states that the number of ISBNs for self-published books has risen by 437 percent between 2008 and 2013.
- Self-publishers are sophisticated at marketing their books, using social media, Amazon, and selling directly from their websites.
- Now print-on-demand books and ebooks can be sold online.
- Self-publishing is gaining respect at last. The Authors Guild now welcomes self-published authors who have earned $5,000 or more from the sale of their books in the previous 18 months.

Clearly, self-publishing is here to stay. The power has shifted to the author who has found a direct path to the reader. There will still be traditional publishers but they will never be able to make that intimate connection that an indie author can make with the person who reads her book. And, think about it: When you finish reading a book that you love, do you remember the book's publisher or the author who wrote it?

CHAPTER NINETEEN

Ethics and Legal Concerns

Ignorance of the law excuses no man.
➤ John Selden [1584–1654]

Plagiarism, copyright infringement, invasion of privacy, and defamation of character, which includes libel and slander, have no place in a book—or anywhere else for that matter. That isn't a moral judgment. It's just plain common sense. We are judged by what we say and what we do. And it may not matter whether we intentionally and knowingly violated a person's rights, stole his words, or damaged his reputation. We can still be sued.

The written word has great power. Once we have put something in writing and sent it out into the world, we can't hit the delete button and get rid of it. Since there's no changing the past, we must make our corrections in the present, or better yet, learn how to avoid making the mistakes in the first place.

It's more than a matter of ethics, what we write has the potential not only to hurt others but to harm ourselves. Our words can come back to haunt us. Very often writers are unaware that they have violated a person's rights or caused consternation or harm. The laws are so complex it isn't always easy to know when we have broken them. But we can become alert to some of the broad rules, including what and where the pitfalls might lie. The following is an examination of some of the things that can get us into trouble.

Defamation

When you injure a person by saying untrue things about him, you have "defamed" him. Defamation by speaking ill of a person is "slander." When lies about a person are written or broadcast it is considered "libel." The difference between the two terms is somewhat muddy but historically it depends on how wide an audience the defamer reached.

Libel is defamation by written or printed words, pictures, or in any form other than by spoken words and gestures; slander is defamation by oral utterance other than by writing, pictures, etc., according to *Webster's New Universal Unabridged Dictionary.*

Some of the elements that are considered in defamation lawsuits are as follows:

- Accuracy. If it is a false statement that does harm to a person, company, product, it is libelous. If it is true, it's not defamatory.
- Opinion. If it is stated as an opinion, not a fact, it is protected under the First Amendment.
- Publication. If the false, injurious statement was shared with a third party, it is considered "published" and therefore libelous.
- Injury. If the lie caused injury to a person's reputation, personal or professional standing, or caused anguish, it is libelous.

Because the dead cannot suffer personally from injury to their reputations, only living people can sue for defamation. And although defamation of the dead is a crime in some states, surviving relatives do not have a right to sue.

Invasion of Privacy

An interference that encroaches on the right to be let alone and to be free from unwanted and unnecessary publicity is considered an invasion of privacy. Invasion of privacy claims generally protect against four distinct types of injury:

- The appropriation of a person's name or likeness for advertising or commercial uses
- The disclosure to the public of embarrassing private facts
- The placing of a person in a false light before the public
- Intrusion into a person's seclusion or private life

The law varies from state to state but most of them require that these invasions of privacy be "highly offensive to a reasonable person" to invoke liability.

The First Amendment can also limit the right to privacy. In fact, the complexity of the doctrines relating to this right make any claim difficult to pursue without legal assistance.

An example of invasion of privacy could be an author's use of a photograph of a person or group of people without their permission. It is always wise to ask them to sign a written release and to offer them at least a small payment as consideration. The following example of a Privacy Release Form can be used with people who pose for you as well as people connected with a piece of writing.

Privacy Release Form

In consideration of ________________________ Dollars ($__________), receipt of which is acknowledged, I, ________________________, do hereby give ________________________, his or her assigns, licensees, and legal representatives the irrevocable right to use my name (or any fictional name), picture, portrait, or photograph in all forms and media and in all manners, including composite or distorted representations, for advertising, trade, or any other lawful purposes, and I waive any right to inspect or approve the finished version(s), including written copy that may be created in connection therewith. I am of full age.* I have read this release and am fully familiar with its contents.

Witness________________ Signed________________
Address________________ Address________________

Date __________, 20____

Consent (if applicable)

I am the parent or guardian of the minor named above and have the legal authority to execute the above release. I approve the foregoing and waive any rights in the premises.

Witness________________ Signed________________
Address________________ Address________________

Date __________, 20____

* Delete this sentence if the subject is a minor. The parent or guardian must then sign the consent.

Fair Use

The owner of copyright has the right to reproduce or to authorize others to reproduce her work. This right, however, is subject to certain limitations. One such limitation is the doctrine of "fair use." A list of the purposes for which the reproduction of a specific work may be considered "fair" is contained in Section 107 of the Copyright Law. Some of them are criticism, comment, news reporting, teaching, and research. In determining whether a use is fair, Section 107 lists four factors to be considered. They are:

1. the purpose and character of the use, including whether such use is of commercial nature or is for nonprofit educational purposes
2. the nature of the copyrighted work
3. the amount and substantiality of the portion used in relation to the copyrighted work as a whole
4. the effect of the use upon the potential market for or value of the copyrighted work

Be aware, however, that the distinction between what is "fair use" and what is infringement cannot be easily defined. Attorney/author Tad Crawford states, "Although everyone who deals with intellectual property seems to have heard of 'fair use,' misconceptions are rife about what the doctrine makes it 'safe' to do."

To quote from Copyright Office FL102 on Fair Use: "There is no specific number of words, lines, or notes that may safely be taken without permission. Acknowledging the source of the copyrighted material does not substitute for obtaining permission."

The following is a sample of a Permission Form. If you are in doubt about whether you can use copyrighted material, it's best to ask for written permission.

Permission Form

The Undersigned hereby grant(s) permission to ______________________________ (hereinafter referred to as the "Author"), located at ______________________________, and to the Author's successors and assigns, to use the material specified in this Permission Form in the book titled ______________________________
to be published by ______________________________
______________________________.

This permission is for the following material:

Nature of material ______________________________

Source ______________________________

Exact description of material, including page numbers______________________________

If published, date of publication ______________________________

Publisher ______________________________

Author(s) ______________________________

This material may be used in the Author's book and in any future revisions, editions, and electronic versions thereof, including nonexclusive world rights in all languages.

It is understood that the grant of this permission shall in no way restrict republication of the material by the Undersigned or others authorized by the Undersigned.

If specified here, the material shall be accompanied on publication by a copyright notice as follows______________________________
and a credit line as follows ______________________________.

Other provisions, if any: ______________________________

If specified here, the requested rights are not controlled in their entirety by the Undersigned and the following owners must be contacted ______________________________
____

One copy of this Permission Form shall be returned to the Author and one copy shall be retained by the Undersigned.

______________________________ ______________________________
Authorized Signatory Date

______________________________ ______________________________
Authorized Signatory Date

Generally, authors, scholars, researchers, and educators may quote small portions of a copyrighted work without getting permission or paying a fee. Examples would be a book reviewer quoting excerpts from a new book or a historian quoting certain passages from an existing work for educational purposes. However, fair use is virtually impossible to determine for sure.

The Copyright Office cannot make the determination of whether a certain use may be considered fair. It cannot give you advice regarding possible copyright violations. And it can't give you permission to use any copyrighted material. You must get permission from the copyright owner.

There is more information on this in *The Writer's Legal Guide: An Authors Guild Desk Reference,* by Tad Crawford and Kay Murray. The Copyright Office provides information on fair use in Circular 21 and FL102. If your question is not clearly answered in any of those publications, you'd best obtain written permission from the owner of the copyright.

This is another case for the rule "When in doubt, take it out," until you either have permission or have consulted with a lawyer who has expertise in this area. Unauthorized use of copyrighted material can be punished by heavy damage awards.

Resources

Books

Associated Press Stylebook and Briefing on Media Law 2014 (www.apstylebook.com).
The AP Stylebook is widely used as a writing and editing reference in newsrooms, classrooms, and corporate offices worldwide.
Bartlett, John. *Bartlett's Familiar Quotations,* 16th edition. Geoffrey O'Brien, General Editor. Little, Brown and Company, 2012.
Books in Print. R.R. Bowker & Co. Published annually.
Bunnin, Brad, and Peter Beren. *The Writer's Legal Companion: the Complete Handbook for the Working Writer.* 3rd edition. Perseus Books, 1998.
The Chicago Manual of Style, 16th edition. The University of Chicago Press. 2010.
Crawford, Tad, Michael Gross and Stevie Fitzgerald. *Business and Legal Forms for Authors and Self-Publishers.* Fourth Edition. Allworth Press, 2015.
Crawford, Tad, and Kay Murray. *The Writer's Legal Guide: An Author's Guild Desk Reference,* Fourth Edition. Allworth Press, 2013.
Forthcoming Books. R.R. Bowker & Co. Published annually.
Guide to Literary Agents. Writer's Digest Books, published annually.
The International Thesaurus of Quotations. HarperPerennial, 1996.
King, Stephen. *On Writing: A Memoir of the Craft.* Pocket Books, 2000.
Lamott, Anne. *Bird by Bird: Some Instructions on Writing and Life.* New York: Anchor Books/Doubleday, 1995.
Larson, Michael. *How to Write a Book Proposal.* Writer's Digest Books, 1997.
Literary Market Place, R.R. Bowker. Published annually.
The New York Public Library Desk Reference. 4th ed. Hyperion, 2002.

The Oxford Dictionary of Quotations. 7th ed. Edited by Elizabeth Knowles. Oxford University Press, 2009.

Poynter, Dan. *The Self-Publishing Manual: How to Write, Print and Sell Your Own Book.* Para Publishing. New editions are released periodically.

Roget, Peter. *Roget's Thesaurus of English Words & Phrases.* 150th Edition. Penguin Books, 2007.

Writer's Market, Where & How to Sell What You Write, Writer's Digest Books. Published annually.

Periodicals

Library Journal, 245 W. 17th Street, New York, NY 10011-5300.

Poets & Writers Inc. 72 Spring St., New York, NY 10012 (bi-monthly magazine for literary writers and poets).

Publishers Weekly (The International News Magazine of Book Publishing and Bookselling) A Cahners/R.R. Bowker Publication.

The Writer, monthly magazine, Kalmbach Publishing Co., 21027 Crossroads Circle, P.O. Box 1612, Waukesha, WI 53187–1612.

Writer's Digest, monthly magazine, F & W Publications, 1507 Dana Avenue, Cincinnati, OH 45207.

Organizations

Check each organization's website for more information regarding their services, membership dues, and any eligibility requirements they may have.

Academy of American Poets. Website: www.poets.org. Supports American poets at all stages of their careers; fosters appreciation of contemporary poetry.

Agent Research & Evaluation. Website: www.agentresearch.com. Tracks agents in court records and the press; publishes a newsletter and sells reports from their database.

American Christian Fiction Writers. Website: www.scfw.com. Critique groups, writing courses, awards, and other resources.

American Crime Writers League. Website: www.acwl.org. Formed to exchange ideas and interact with other writers.

American Screenwriters Association. Website: www.asascreenwriters.com. Promotion and encouragement of the art of screenwriting.

American Society of Journalists & Authors, Inc. Website: www.asja.org. Writers association of independent nonfiction writers.

Association of Authors' Representatives, Inc. (AAR). Website: www.aaronline.org. A not-for-profit membership organization of literary and dramatic agents. Member agents must meet professional standards specified in the organization's bylaws and agree to subscribe to its Canon of Ethics.

The Authors Guild. Website: www.authorsguild.org. Advocate for writers' interests in effective copyright protection, fair contracts and free expression. Provides legal assistance and a broad range of web services to its members.

Christian Writers Guild. Website: www.christianwritersguild.com

Historical Novel Society. Website: www.historicalnovelsociety.org. Provides support and opportunities for new writers of historical fiction.

International Thriller Writers. Website: www.thrillerwriters.org

Mystery Writers of America. Website: www.mysterywriters.org. Sponsors conferences, presents Edgar Awards, and provides information for mystery writers.

National Association of Women Writers. Website: www.naww.org. "Where women unite to write."

National Writers Association. Website: www.nationalwriters.com. Provides education and an ethical resource for writers at all levels of experience.

National Writers Union. Website: www.nwu.org. A labor union committed to improving the working conditions of freelance writers.

PEN American Center. Website: www.pen.org. Membership consists of playwrights, essayists, editors, and novelists.

Poetry Society of America. Website: www.poetrysociety.org. Offers support for all poets from professionals to unpublished writers.

Romance Writers of America. Website: rwanational.org. Provide opportunities to share experiences with other writers.

Science Fiction & Fantasy Writers of America, Inc. Website: www.sfwa.org. Nonprofit writers association that brings together writers of speculative fiction.

Small Publishers Association of North America (SPAN). Website: www.spannet.org. Supports self-publishing authors and small publishers as a nonprofit trade association.

Society of Children's Book Writers and Illustrators. Website: www.scbwi.org. Offers a variety of services to people who write, illustrate, or are interested in children's literature.

Writers Guild of America-East (New York). Website: www.wgae.org. A labor union representing professional writers in the motion picture, broadcast, cable, and new media industries. Members must be published or employed in the field.

Writers Guild of America-West (California). Website: www.wga.org. (See above description) Both WGAE and WGAW provide a registration service for literary material.

The above lists of resources are only a few that are available to authors. There are many valuable publications and organizations that offer specific help. Your goals, needs, specialty, and location will determine which ones are right for you.

Glossary

acknowledgment	An expression of appreciation.
acquisitions editor	The person at a book publishing company in charge of acquiring product; usually the person to whom a query or book proposal is sent.
active voice	A voice of verbal inflection in which the subject of the sentence is represented as performing the action expressed by the verb: *she will always remember her first love; he hit the ball.*
adjective	Any of a class of words used to modify a noun by limiting, qualifying, or specifying. It is distinguished by having comparative and superlative endings like *-able, -ous, -er, –est.* An adjective describes or specifies the quantity or quality of a noun.
advance	Money paid to an author by a publisher prior to publication. An advance is paid against royalties.
adverb	Any of a class of words distinguished by the ending *–ly* or by functioning as a modifier of verbs or clauses, adjectives, or other adverbs or adverbial phrases, such as *very, well, quickly.*
agent	A person authorized to act on another's behalf. Agents are paid on a percentage basis. Literary agents working with authors of books usually get 15 percent; script agents who work with scriptwriters usually get 10 percent.
almanac	An annual reference book of useful and interesting facts.

analogy	A similarity between like features of two things, a comparison; usually followed by *to, with,* or *between.*
antagonist	A major character opposing the protagonist
back matter	Elements of a book that follow the text, such as appendix, index, glossary, list of resources, bibliography, and author biography.
bar code	A set of short, vertical lines and spaces printed on a product, designed to be machine readable to yield a price, ISBN, etc. Required by most retailers.
bestseller	Books that sell in large quantities; based on sales by bookstores, wholesalers, and/or distributors
bibliography	A list of source materials such as books and articles used in the preparation of a book or referred to in the text.
binding	Pages of a book bound together with thread, staples, adhesive, or other means.
blog	Short for Web log, a list of journal entries posted on a Web page.
blueline	(Also called blues) a paper print made from a single negative, used primarily as a proof, to check content and/or positioning.
book review	A critical appraisal of a book often reflecting a reviewer's personal opinion and/or recommendation.
Books in Print	Listings of books currently in print, published by R. R. Bowker, providing ordering information including titles, authors, publishers, ISBNs, binding (hardcover or paperback), and prices.
bundle of rights	A copyright that provides authors, music composers, and creators of artistic works the sole right to grant or refuse permission to use their copyrighted works.
case bound	Book bound in a rigid material; also known as hardcover.
casing	Alternate term for binding.
character	A person represented in a story, drama, etc.
chronology	Determination of dates and sequence of events; arrangements of events in time.
CIP	Cataloging-in-Publication: a cataloging record prepared to the standards of the Library of Congress which enables libraries to catalog titles.

cliché	A trite, stereotyped expression; a platitude.
coauthor	One of two or more joint authors; to write in joint authorship.
collaboration	Working with one another; cooperation; as writers collaborating to produce a book.
comb binding	Mechanical binding using a plastic spring-like comb that fits through holes punched in the edges of pages.
concept	A general notion or idea.
consistency	Adherence to the same principles, course, or form; uniformity.
content editor	Person who evaluates the flow, logic and overall message of a manuscript.
continuity	A continuous or connected whole.
copyeditor	Person who does line by line editing to correct errors in spelling, grammar, consistency, punctuation, etc.
copyright	A legal right granted to an author, composer, or artist for exclusive publication, production, sale, or distribution of a literary, musical or artistic work for a specified period of time.
cover letter	A brief explanatory letter that accompanies a manuscript or book proposal.
deadline	Author's due date for delivery of the completed manuscript to the publisher.
defamation	False or unjustified injury of another's good reputation, as by slander or libel.
desktop publishing	Creating and composing pages including text and graphics on a computer.
distributor	A firm that stocks, promotes, sells, and distributes materials.
dust jacket	A printed wrapper, usually paper, placed around a casebound book.
edit	To revise or correct, as a manuscript.
editor	A person who edits material for a publication; a manager or supervisor for a publication such as a book publishing company, newspaper, or magazine. (see copyeditor and content editor)
electronic publishing	The process of using a computer to enter both text and graphics and to integrate them for final output.
end sheets	The pages at the beginning and end of a book that are pasted against the inside board of the case; also called endpapers, endleaves, or lining paper.

epigraph	A quotation at the beginning of a literary composition that suggests the theme.
epilogue	A short concluding section at the end of a literary work.
ethics	Moral principles or values.
ethnic	Characteristic of a people or group sharing a common and distinctive culture, religion, or language.
Facebook	A social networking website.
fiction	The class of literature comprising works of imaginative narration.
flow	To proceed continuously, smoothly, or easily.
flyleaf	A blank page at the beginning or end of a book.
font	A complete assortment of type of one style and size.
foreword	Part of the front matter of a book; a short introductory statement usually written by someone other than the author, often an authority on the subject of the book.
format	The general appearance of a book such as typeface, margins, binding, etc.
front matter	The elements that precede the text of a book, such as the title page, copyright page, dedication, table of contents, foreword, preface, introduction, and acknowledgments.
galley	Printed proof of text copy before being made into pages, often used for proofreading or presentation reviews.
genre	A class or category of artistic endeavor having a particular form, content, technique, or the like
ghostwriter	A person who writes for another person who is presumed to be the author.
gutter	Inner margin of each page, from printing to binding.
hardcover	Book bound in a rigid material; also known as case bound.
idiomatic	Peculiar to or characteristic of a particular language or dialect: *idiomatic expression*; having a distinctive style, esp. in the arts: *idiomatic writing.*
infelicity	Something inappropriate.
infringement	A violation as of a law or agreement.
Internet	An interconnected system of networks that connects computers around the world.
introduction	A preliminary part of a book leading up to the main part and written by the author. It may be

	extensive and is usually printed as part of the text.
ISBN	International Standard Book Number: the International standard numbering system for the information industry; required for books sold through bookstores.
jargon	Specialized language of a trade, profession, or similar group.
LCCN	Library of Congress Card Number: a pre-assigned card number issued by the Library of Congress. A unique identification number assigned to the catalog record created for each book in its catalogued collections.
leaf	A sheet of paper in a book; a page is one side of a leaf.
leaves	Trimmed sheets of paper that make up a book.
libel	A defamatory statement.
Library of Congress	One of the major library collections in the world, located in Washington, D.C., and functioning as the national library of the United States, though not officially designated as such.
license	Official or legal permission to do or own a specified thing.
Literary Market Place (LMP)	Annual directory of the publishing industry that contains a comprehensive list of publishers and publishing-allied listings, such as literary agencies, writer's conferences, wholesalers, distributors, etc.
margins	The unprinted space between the text and the edge of the page.
metaphor	A figure of speech in which a term or phrase is applied to something to which it is not literally applicable in order to suggest a resemblance.
narrative	A story or account of events, experiences, or the like, whether true or fictitious.
nonfiction	All writing or books not fiction, poetry, or drama; the broadest category of written works.
noun	Any member of a class or words that can function as the main or only elements of subjects or objects. Nouns refer to persons, places, things, states, or qualities.
novel	A fictitious prose narrative of considerable length and complexity, portraying characters and presenting a sequential organization of action and scenes.
paperback	A book with a flexible paper binding.

PCIP	Publisher's Cataloging in Publication; a service of Quality Books Inc. Provides librarians with information needed to determine shelf location in libraries.
passive voice	A voice of verbal inflection in which the subject of the sentence is the object of the action rather than causing the action: *The ball was hit by him.*
perfect bound	The binding usually used on a paperback book where the cover is glued into place.
person	In grammar, a category used to distinguish between the speaker of an utterance and those to or about whom he is speaking. In English there are three persons in the pronouns: first person, *I* and *we;* second person, *you;* third person, *he, she, it, they.*
plagiarism	The unauthorized use of the language and thoughts of another author while representing them as one's own work.
plot	Also called storyline; the plan or main story of a novel or short story.
preface	The author's own statement, often including acknowledgments. It follows the foreword if there is one and is part of the front matter of a book.
proofread	To read and mark corrections in a manuscript.
protagonist	The leading character.
public domain	Published material that is available for use without the need to obtain permission, either because it has not been copyrighted or has a copyright that has expired.
publisher	The company or entity that prepares printed material for public distribution or sale.
punctuation	The use of standard signs and marks in writing to separate words into sentences, clauses, and phrases in order to clarify meaning.
query letter	A letter, usually no more than one page long in which a writer proposes an article or book idea; written to an agent or publisher asking for either representation or publication of the author's writing.
recto	The front of the leaf (page), the side that lies to the right in an open book; an odd-numbered page.
saddle stitch	A binding that fastens pages together with wires (resembling staples) through the middle fold of the sheets.

SASE	Self-addressed stamped envelope.
simile	A figure of speech in which two unlike things are explicitly compared.
spine	The back of a bound book connecting the front and back covers; also called backbone.
spiral bound	A type of mechanical binding using a continuous wire of corkscrew or spring coil form that runs through holes punched in the binding edge.
story	Narration of an event or series of events.
synopsis	A general view; a brief narrative description of the book, usually one or two pages in length.
tense	A set of tense forms indicating a particular time. Example: past tense, *I saw the painting*; present tense, *I see the painting;* future tense, *I will see the painting.*
theme	An idea, point of view, or perception.
thesaurus	A book of synonyms and antonyms.
transition	Passage from one subject to another.
treatment	In screenwriting, a synopsized narration of the story, action, and dialogue; usually containing more pages than a synopsis for a book.
trim size	The finished size of a book after trimming.
tweet	an online posting on Twitter.
Twitter	A real-time information network for sharing what's happening now.
verb	Part of speech that expresses action, existence, or occurrence.
verso	The back of the leaf (page), the side that lies to the left when the leaf is turned; an even-numbered page.
wholesaler	A company that takes orders, buys from publishers or distributors, and sells to retailers.
word wrap	Also called wraparound: a word processing feature that automatically spills text from one line to the next without manually inserting line returns.

Index